GILLIES OF PARTICK

To David e Fena
with the Lord's richest
blessing
Kenny Gillies

D1363162

Rev. Kenneth Gillies, Partick Gardner Street Church of Scotland, 1924–1976.

GILLIES OF PARTICK

The Life and Ministry of an Applecross Man

K. A. Gillies

Cagey Lad Publishing

Published by Cagey Lad Publishing
            17 Craigmaroinn Gardens
            Aberdeen
            AB12 3SG
            Tel: (01224) 879768
            e-mail: gillieskl@cageylad.freeserve.co.uk

IBSN 0 9536799 O X

Printed in Scotland by Claymore Graphics Limited, Aberdeen.

Dedicated
to the
Memory
of
Hector J Gillies
(1928 - 94)
a beloved uncle
who shared not only
his father's faith
but also his sense of humour

Foreword

This is a very interesting account of the life and work of the Reverend Kenneth Gillies who, in my opinion, was an outstanding witness for the Lord Jesus Christ whom he loved and served so well in his beloved Highlands, in the Partick Community of Glasgow, and beyond. He was, to say the least, a charming but unusual character.

I first encountered Kenneth in 1946 when I was a young uniformed police officer working in Partick. I spotted this big man striding along Dumbarton Road towards Gardner Street dressed in a very long black raincoat, dark suit, clerical collar and black homburg hat. Indeed, I cannot remember him in any other garb except when the weather was too hot for a coat. During his walk he would stop and look around as if inspecting what was happening in the vicinity, or checking to ensure that he wasn't being followed. I later learned that this trait probably came from his police training. He had been a constable in the Partick Burgh Police - which later became part of Glasgow City Police - about forty years before I joined the force. It was this, together of course with our evangelical faith, which caused us to become good friends.

But Kenneth Gillies was not just a big man physically, he was a giant of a man spiritually. He had, as this book relates, a long and distinguished ministry in Partick Gardner Street Church, but it did not end there. He was involved in many aspects of Church outreach such as the "All Scotland Crusade" in 1955 with Billy Graham, and the ongoing activities of the Glasgow United Evangelistic Association and, in particular, the work of the Tent Hall. Individuals and Churches faithfully attempting to preach the gospel and extend the Kingdom had Kenneth's support.

I often met Kenneth and shared the platform with him at the Tent Hall. On many occasions he was asked to pray and believe me this was an experience. It was most obvious that he spent a lot of time in communion with his Lord and when he prayed in public he took the congregation straight into the presence of the Almighty. I for one was left in no doubt that he was 'far ben' with his Lord and was a regular at the Throne of Grace.

Kenneth Gillies during his long ministry influenced many with his words of wisdom and encouraging advice. Denominational barriers did not concern him; he had a warm welcome for all his brothers and sisters in Christ. And this is how it ought to be!

This big man, who lived a quite wonderful life which lasted almost nine decades, will be remembered as a prayer warrior, an encourager, and one who never missed an opportunity to tell others about Christ. But, over and above all of these, those who knew him best will retain the memory of his faithfulness. It could be said of Kenneth that his life manifested the faith he had in the Master he served so well.

I am certain of this - we will not see his like again.

Sir David McNee, Glasgow
Commissioner (Retired), Metropolitan Police
Formerly Chief Constable, City of Glasgow Police

Preface

It was his hands that grabbed you first. Fascinating hands. Big and strong with the skin pulled taut over them. Hands which enveloped yours in the warmth of their greeting. Hands which belonged to the one whom my sister, brother and I were privileged to know simply as 'Grandpa'.

We looked forward to our holidays in the Beechwood manse (even if it didn't have a TV!) and to his visits to our home in Tongue, Sutherland. We enjoyed his teasing and benefited from his generosity. Laughter was never far away when he was around and neither would he part from us without placing a "penny" into our grateful hands. Like his Master, he drew children to himself and sought to bless them.

We respected his devotion to God for his life manifested true holiness and godliness. In my mind's eye, I can still see him in the drawing-room of the manse singing one of his favourite psalms, Psalm 121, the words of which reflect the trust he had in the Lord's faithfulness, protection and love.

I to the hills will lift mine eyes,
From whence doth come mine aid.
My safety cometh from the Lord,
Who heaven and earth hath made.
The Lord shall keep thy soul,
He shall preserve thee from all ill.
Henceforth thy going out and in,
God keep forever will.

In working on this book over the past three years, my appreciation of my grandfather's life and ministry has been greatly expanded. This has been due in no small part to all those who so willingly took the time to either write or talk to me about him. Each and every reminiscence whether big or small proved valuable in enhancing my impression of who he was and what he meant to so many.

Additionally, there are a number of people whose instrumental help during the writing of this biography I would like to specifically acknowledge. These are:-

My father, Alexander, for his enthusiasm and encouragement throughout this project; and for having the foresight to keep a diary from childhood!

My wife, Lynne, whose practical and moral support continues to be a source of great strength and love.

Kenneth D. MacDonald, former Session Clerk in Gardner Street, whose insights and comments at various stages were extremely helpful; and for the vital work of translating Gaelic sermons and tributes.

The Rev. Duncan Mackinnon, latterly Church of Scotland minister at Kyle, and Archie Macleod, former elder in Gardner Street, for their significant contributions, too, in translating Gaelic material. The latter's extensive personal recollections were also especially notable.

The Rev. Roderick Morrison and the Kirk Session of Gardner Street Church of Scotland for the unlimited access to the several volumes of relevant church records.

Iain and Mary MacLeod for their hospitality and friendship in accommodating me on my visits to Glasgow.

Steve and Áine Collins, together with Peter Kiehlmann, for kindnesses and expertise in the realm of computer technology.

I would also like to thank staff at the following locations for their professional help and advice in the course of my research:-

Aberdeen Central Library; Aberdeen University Dept. of Special Collections and Archives; Aberdeen University Queen Mother Library; Admiralty Library, London; Glasgow Bible College; Inverness Public Library; Mitchell Library, Glasgow; National Library of Scotland, Edinburgh; Scottish Records Office, Edinburgh.

Lastly, Proverbs 3:6 calls us to acknowledge the Lord God in all our ways. Gladly, therefore, I thank Him for His initiative, inspiration, and guidance in the writing of this book. My ultimate prayer is that the grace and glory of Jesus would be seen through its testimony.

Kenny Gillies, Aberdeen
July 1999

Contents

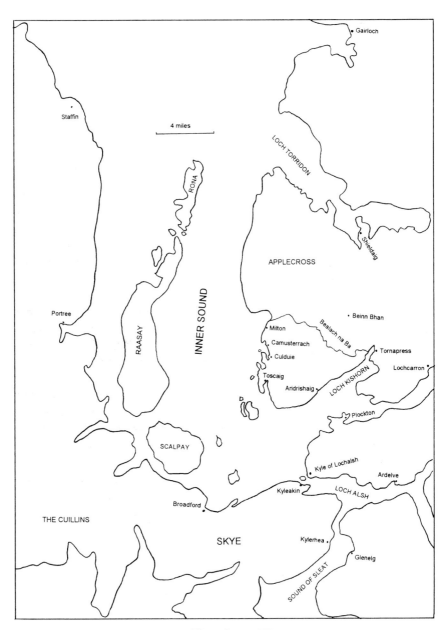

Wester Ross and Skye

Chapter 1

Applecross Background

On the furthermost margin of Wester Ross lies the mountainous region of Applecross. Shaped by the sea lochs of Torridon in the north and Kishorn in the south the only road into this remote area until some twenty years ago was over the Bealach na Ba (Pass of the Cow), winding Alpine-like from sea level to an ear-popping 2,054 feet. Bounded by crash barriers at the most vulnerable points, this single-track road weaves upwards for a distance of six miles through wild and dramatic scenery until the rock-strewn summit is reached. Here, when the mist is not enveloping the mountain-top, a panoramic view of the islands of Skye, Raasay, and Rona across the Inner Sound spreads out before the traveller. On an especially clear day, the outline of the distant Outer Hebrides can also be made out far to the north-west whilst, nearer at hand, the hog's-back of Beinn Bhàn looms impressively. Descending from the top, the road continues to twist and turn this way and that, though somewhat less tortuously, before arriving at the first of the many townships found scattered along the Applecross seaboard.

Three miles to the south of where the hill road ends lies Culduie, a collection of a dozen or so buildings for the most part strung out like pearls along the neck of the hillside.[1] A stone dyke, like some rectangular garland, provides a hedge for the thirty to forty acres of croftland which flows down from this line of houses. It was here that Kenneth Gillies was born on July 25, 1887.

Named after his maternal grandfather, Kenneth was Alexander and Catherine Gillies' third child. Married for six years they already had a son, John, and a daughter, Chirsty. Kenneth's father was a tall, well built man - known as Ali Bàn because of his fair hair - who once demonstrated the hardy side of his character when he rowed his uncle's sixteen-foot boat all the way from Ardelve, on the shores of Loch Alsh, to Culduie.

Primarily dependent for his livelihood upon the sea, Ali Bàn not only managed to deal with the varied demands of being a fisherman but, like most of his contemporaries, was also able to turn his hand to planting crops, handling livestock, repairing and building. Within any crofting township the sharing together of these skills was vital if the families in the community were to graft out a living in often hard circumstances. Even so, there were still times when Ali Bàn had to leave home to find seasonal work on farms in the east.

Catherine Gillies, Kenneth's mother, was a tall, stately woman, noted for her gracious disposition and kindness to all. A Matheson from the township of Milton, she was a person of conspicuous godliness who provided the spiritual leadership in the family home. This was the case because her husband did not profess faith in Christ until near the end of his life. The influence of godly mothers on their offspring down through history has been noted

1

Culduie, 1953. The Gillies family home is circled.

and could include such as Hannah and Samuel, Monica and St. Augustine, Susannah Wesley with John and Charles, to name but a few.[2]

The house Kenneth was brought up in was a black house, a type of house which still predominated in the West Highlands and Islands during the latter part of the nineteenth century. Constructed of stone with a heather-thatched roof, the single-storey building's three rooms each had a small window. Located on the earth floor in one of the gable ends was a fireplace which had hanging above it a hook for kettles and the like. Later, the fire was set higher with a grate. There may not have been much in the way of space or comfort for the Gillies family but, then, "the Gael has always been an outdoor man. 'Home' to him was the great outdoors, and his home was merely a convenient shelter from inclement weather. It was not an object of domestic luxury. Rather, it was a building erected to shut out the storm."[3]

The croft at No.8 Culduie extended to three acres, allowing a handful of sheep and black cattle to be kept, and on which there were small plots of oats, barley, and potatoes. During the winter months, salt herring and potatoes were the staple fare although eggs from a few hens gave some variety to the diet.

Also rented by Ali Bàn was Eilean an Naoimh (Saint Island). Situated a few hundred yards off the point of Ard Dhubh, it was capable of taking six to eight sheep for summer grazing. St. Maelrubha, one of the Irish monks who followed in the wake of St. Columba, is reputed to have first landed on the island prior to his establishing a monastery at

Looking west towards the Cuillins from behind Culduie, 1953.

Applecross in A.D. 673. The ancient Gaelic name for Applecross, A'Chomraich (The Sanctuary), signifying immunity and protection from prosecution or punishment, stems from this time.

The association between Culduie and the Gillies family had first begun some fifty years before Kenneth's birth with the arrival in the hamlet of his great-grandfather, Alexander Gillies (Ali Ruadh). His settlement in 1837 from Aridrishaig, on the south-eastern coast of Applecross, followed an exchange of houses with a shepherd by the name of Bain. The arrangement, however, was by no means mutual for the shepherd had used his connections with the estate factor to get access to the better grazings at Aridrishaig. Consequently, Ali Ruadh, at over sixty years of age, was left with no alternative but to move to Culduie, accompanied by his younger brother, Duncan, and their respective families. This must have been an especially dispiriting situation in the light of the fact that the family had previously been evicted some years earlier from land near Tornapress, a few miles along the shore of Loch Kishorn.

Culduie was one of those inhospitable places where people had been forced to go in the wake of clearances from the fertile land around the river Applecross in the early 1800's.[4] These events had taken place at the instigation of John MacKenzie, the 7th Laird of Applecross, a man "who earned himself a very unsavoury local reputation through his enthusiastic enforcement of...estate improvement and [its] corollary of eviction."[5] As repeated victims of estate policy themselves, Ali Ruadh and his family were thus forced to

3

make the best they could from a stony, bog-strewn ground and an often unwelcoming sea. Shelter, too, was a necessity. Writing in 1836, the Rev. Roderick Macrae noted, "the climate is rather moist and foggy, and torrents of rain frequently fall in all seasons of the year."[6]

The Gillies' arrival in Culduie occurred at a time when the preferred option for many in Applecross was emigration. Between 1831 and 1839, it was recorded that "20 to 30 families...emigrated to the British colonies of North America."[7] There were several factors which contributed to this state of affairs including high rents, no security of tenure, miserable housing, a scarcity of peat, and the failure of the herring fishing.[8]

The Gillies' stayed put, however, and in the decades which followed their presence steadily grew. So much so, that by 1891, four years after Kenneth was born, half the ten dwellings in Culduie were occupied by relatives of his. Next door (No.9) was his father's brother, Duncan, and his family; on the other side (No.7) was his late grandfather's first cousin, Chirsty, married to John MacIntosh from Lochalsh; two doors further down (No.5) lived his great-uncle Donald and his family; and residing at the north end of Culduie (No.2) was his widowed grandmother, Mary, and her spinster daughter, Barbara. Out of fifty or so folk in the township around a third were surnamed Gillies. Not surprisingly, a great deal of interaction took place between the various houses and, as one of maybe a dozen children, Kenneth had a fair number of friends in the immediate vicinity with whom he could play including his cousins next door, John, Alasdair (Mòr) and Colin.

Kenneth attended Applecross Public School which was situated in the neighbouring township of Camusterrach. His schoolmaster, John Matheson, originally from Plockton, had been at the school since coming from Caithness in 1875.

Mr Matheson's relationship with both parents and pupils alike was somewhat turbulent. His fiery red beard was evidently matched by a fiery temper! This led to a series of complaints being made to the School Board in August 1899, by a number of parents who were "dissatisfied with [him] as a teacher and for using abusive language to the pupils."[9]

This was not the first time, unfortunately, that Mr Matheson had been in bother. Indeed, in the previous year he had been asked to resign by the School Board due to the "backward state of the Applecross School...[and]...hopeless to expect improvement under the present teacher."[10] However, on appeal, the Board relented and decided to leave him at his post. In this latest episode, Mr Matheson was warned that the abusive language had to cease and a decision was made to employ a woman assistant to help "with the infants, lower standards, and to teach needlework."[11] The Free Church minister, the Rev. Kenneth Macdonald, a native of the parish who would gain a wide audience with his book *Social and Religious Life in the Highlands,* dissented from the decision to retain Mr Matheson and protested that it was "against the wishes of the parents...[and]...unjust to retain the services of a man who has been found guilty of the charges."[12] Nevertheless, Mr Matheson was able to weather the storm and remained there until his retirement in 1907.

A schoolboy contemporary of Kenneth's, William Murchison from Toscaig, relates in

Kenneth's parents, Alexander and Catherine Gillies, flanked by neighbours Jessie Gillies (left) and Bella MacPherson, 1933.

his book *Master in Sail* what it was like to be taught during these years by the man nicknamed 'Geordie' by his pupils.

"None of us, of course, could speak English. The school was there to teach, and when we were out playing the schoolmaster would tell us to speak English in the Playtime, but nobody did, and some of the wild boys would defy the schoolmaster, and they were thrashed for not speaking English...the older boys were a frequent source of trouble to the schoolmaster...I have seen him getting hold of them in their seats and hauling them out on the floor to be thrashed. They would hang on to the seats and he would lose his temper; but for the fact that the seats were bolted to the floors, boys, seats and all would have been out on the middle of the floor. They would be kept in for disobeying orders, but immediately he left the school for his house for afternoon tea, they would open the window and jump out and run home. The school, very often, was a tug of war, and looking back on it, I often wonder how any order came out of such chaos."[13] Captain Murchison concludes, "most of the boys did well later on in life...which shows that early education is not of such importance after all."(!)

School holidays were from mid-to-late August through to the end of September or first week of October. This was a busy time for the community as both the harvest and fishing season were at their peak and Kenneth was expected to play his part. During the spring time, too, he would have stayed at home for up to a fortnight to help plant the potatoes.

Captain Murchison's recollections give a first-hand insight into what was typical work in a Wester Ross township at this time and recalls how his father worked the càs-chrom (foot-plough):

5

"I followed him putting the potatoes in the row, and also seaweed, sometimes with a mixture of cow dung. Mother would also be busy carrying some of the seaweed in a creel on her back and also the cow manure. Also Mother cut the potatoes for planting. In those days it would be the height of extravagance to put down or plant a full potato as seed. One potato was carefully examined and cut into small pieces according to the number of eyes that looked good for planting."[14]

In Culduie, Kenneth's father collected seaweed from Saint Island and transported it to the shore in his twenty-foot open boat called The *Crofter*. It was then unloaded and carted up to the croft using creels.

Towards the end of April, after the spring work was finished, peat cutting would begin. Ali Bàn's peat bank was situated well up the hill directly behind his house. Whether "peat cutting, peat lifting, stacking or [taking] them home we went out for the whole day - in other words, if the weather was favourable, we seldom got home before 7pm, in time for supper and bed for tired boys."[15]

Work and play, nevertheless, ceased on a Sunday. Like the majority of the community in the 1890's, the Gillies family belonged to the Free Church of Scotland. Like the school, the church was in Camusterrach, a mile north of Culduie.

"Going to church was the order of the day, every Sunday, and there were no conveyances except one's legs...morning and evening services...the minister normally took 2½ hours to preach and complete the service...[and]...very often it was damnation and hell and the terrors and torments for those who did not believe."[16]

The influence of the church upon the community was nothing if not profound through its solemn and often stern religiosity. A contrast in some ways from a people who, in spite of not having much in terms of material possessions, were of a largely sociable and happy disposition.

Life for Kenneth Gillies and his family, nonetheless, had its fair share of sorrows. His younger brothers, Roddy and Duncan, were born in 1890 and 1895 respectively but, sadly, Duncan suffered from hydrocephalus and died only seven months old. The following year, February 27, 1897, tragedy once again struck the Gillies household when Kenneth's twelve-year old sister, Chirsty, died in her father's arms after succumbing to an attack of asthma. She had suffered much in previous years from the effects of tuberculosis. What increases the poignancy of her death, however, was the fact that just a few hours previously her sister, Annie Mary, had been born. One can only imagine the heightened and conflicting emotions which must have surged through the family that day. The contrast between joy and relief, on the one hand, and pain and distress, on the other, must have been desperate. Life and death, hope and despair, side-by-side.

By the time Kenneth was twelve or thirteen his involvement with the sea was well under way. A report around this time refers to the fact that in Applecross "the fishing is of considerable importance and many of the crofters possess boats of the Loch Fyne type of skiff with which they fish in the West Highland lochs for a portion of the year."[17]

At first, Kenneth's fishing trips would have been limited to setting herring nets close to home from boats such as The *Crofter*. The nets being then lifted early the following morning and the fish transported to market in Kyleakin or Kyle of Lochalsh. On leaving school he would certainly have had experience of the bigger Loch Fyne type of skiffs such as the *Bella* which his father and uncle jointly owned. These boats were some twenty-five foot in length, fitted out with a sailing mast and oars, and covered with a deck about a third of the way. Each boat had a crew of four and when required Kenneth would act as relief for one or other of the men. After the herring season finished in November the fisherman went after white fish such as whiting and ling, frequently sailing to Raasay.

This dependence on the seasonal variabilities of fishing led at times to economic hardship in the community. In a letter written in early 1903 by Donald Mackenzie, District Clerk of Applecross Parish Council, regarding the proposed construction of new footpaths in the area, he argues passionately that "on account of the complete failure of the herring fishing in the past season, and the consequent straitened circumstances of the people...employment of the fishermen on the works would very materially relieve their exceptionally impoverished condition."[18] Some months later, Kenneth was one of the local men taken on to help build these gravel paths to the southern Applecross townships of Ard Dhubh, Collieghillie, Ardbain, and Camusteil, the first two of which were seen as "by far the most necessitous places."[19] One of his co-labourers was Roddy Murchison, brother of the aforementioned Captain and himself later to have the same title.

Subsidised by a 75% grant from the Congested Districts Board with the remainder being contributed by Lord Middleton, the estate proprietor, the work was almost complete by the following spring when it was commended as "excellently done...and...of great benefit to the people."[20] The physical nature of these early years working on the croft, in the boats, and on the roads, was to give Kenneth a reservoir of muscular strength which would serve him well for the rest of his life.

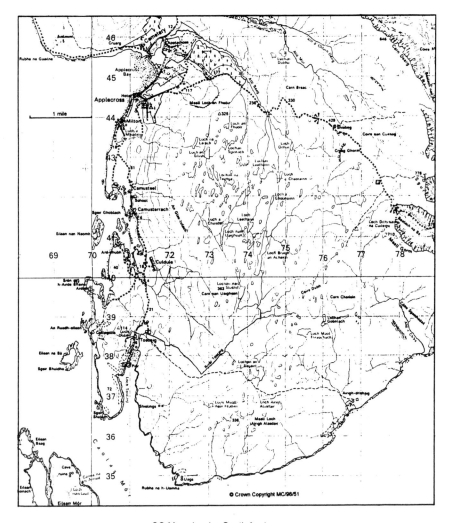

OS Map showing South Applecross

Chapter 2

New Directions

The beginning of 1904 brought more tragic news to the Gillies household with the death of Kenneth's older brother, John, following a ruptured appendix. He had been training to be a mason in Glasgow and had intended returning to Culduie to build a house for his parents when his apprenticeship finished. He was aged just twenty-two. It was another distressing blow for the family to endure, particularly when they had already suffered so grievously through the loss of both Chirsty and Duncan.

The next winter almost brought further disaster when Kenneth's only surviving brother, Roddy, was caught in a snowstorm taking the mail to the isolated townships of Aridrishaig and Uags. A search party was sent out but, thankfully, he made it back home safely. One can only speculate how uptight the family must have been at the thought of losing a fourth member.

Shortly after this incident, Kenneth - like so many other young Highlanders both before and after him - headed south to Glasgow in search of work. He soon found employment with the Allan Shipping Line and spent some time traversing the North Atlantic as a crew member on their vessels. After a couple of years of doing this, however, he decided to get his feet back on dry land and embarked on a career change which would soon lead him in a completely different direction.

On May 20, 1907, Kenneth signed up with the Partick Burgh Police.[1] Serving alongside him, of course, were several other Gaelic-speaking officers including one with the same name from Snizort in Skye. A few months later Kenneth was also to be joined by one of his schoolfriends from Culduie, Duncan Gillanders.

Just short of his twentieth birthday and standing 6'2" tall, Police Constable Gillies was to build up a good solid reputation for himself during the course of the next two years. His handsome looks soon earned him the nickname of "Bonnie Bobbie", whilst his standard of physical fitness meant that when off-duty he was able to enter - with some degree of success - various wrestling competitions.

Living and working in a community which had a strong Highland influence, Kenneth "was glad to be away from the restraints of a religious upbringing, no longer under obligation to attend a place of worship."[2] Nonetheless, on one Sunday evening, October 22, 1908, he was to attend a service which was to irrevocably change his life. Andrew Woolsey, in an article to mark Kenneth Gillies' fifty years in the ministry, picks up the story of that night when he stepped into Partick Gardner Street United Free Church.

"Glancing round, he quickly spotted an empty seat in full view of the pulpit and settled himself for the service. Normally a retiring lad, who preferred to remain

The young Highlander in Glasgow, 1905.

in the background, Kenneth Gillies was anxious tonight that the minister would see him.

Not that he was particularly interested in what ministers had to say but...the minister from Applecross, the Rev. Angus MacIver, had come to assist at the Communion services...and realising that his mother would be inquiring of the minister when he returned if Kenneth had been at the services, Kenneth considered it prudent to make an appearance.

Just once! The last service too! It wouldn't last long! In any case, he was on night duty and would have to leave before it was over! But, as the sermon commenced, Kenneth became absorbed in the simple, clear presentation of the gospel. Mr MacIver was commenting on Rev. 3:20: *Behold, I stand at the door and knock: if any man hear my voice, and open the door, I will come in to him, and will sup with him, and he with me.*

Is that the way to salvation? Can it be so simple? Only a step from death to life? Why hadn't he seen it before? Kenneth Gillies never hesitated. There and then he yielded his life to the Saviour and crossed the threshold. He glanced at his watch. Time for the beat. Quietly he rose from his seat, and left the church - a new man in Christ!"[3]

Soon after, Kenneth wrote to Mr MacIver telling him what had happened. The minister responded by sending a letter which Kenneth was to treasure for the rest of his days.

United Free Manse
Applecross
November 5, 1908

My Dear Kenny,

I praise God for the letter you wrote me, and which I received last night. There is nothing in this life so important as a decision for Christ. Although there would be nothing else in my going to Partick it would be well worth my while to go to be the means in God's hand of guiding one soul to the Saviour. One soul is of more value than the whole world, and the Lord Jesus Christ gave His own life to redeem us. And now Kenny that He has showed you that He is gracious do not be ashamed to do His will, to confess His name. As a good soldier of Jesus Christ don't be ashamed of your colours, or of your Captain, and may the Lord bless you very abundantly. I cannot tell you how delighted I am with your letter, and I pray God that you may be a blessing to others. Let Jesus sup with you now and you will sup with Him afterwards. Remember your Bible and your prayers.

I was in Culduie yesterday. We had the meeting in John MacPherson's house. I was speaking to your mother, and told her you were well. She will be pleased to hear that you have given yourself to the Lord. He is the Good Shepherd, and is able to keep you. I think Kenny if you have not written your mother about this, you should write. It will be such gladness to her heart.

The friends here are well, and there is nothing new to write about. The greatest and best news are to hear of people being saved. And now with love from us all to "my son in the faith" of Christ Jesus.

I am yours very sincerely
Angus MacIver

PS Your mother came to see me. She tells me you wrote Roderick about it. She says that nothing in the world could give her so much joy as the news of your conversion does. And Roderick could not tell his mother about what was in the letter with tears and weeping with joy. I hope the news will be blessed to Roderick himself. Jesus is "mighty to save".

Seven months later Kenneth resigned from the police despite the best efforts to dissuade him by the Burgh Superintendent, William Cameron, who was also a member in Gardner Street Church. Neither the prospect of promotion nor an increase in his weekly wage of 27/5d were going to distract him from the calling of God upon his life. Nevertheless, he was to retain a great affection for the police and, in the years to come, took an active interest in the spiritual well-being of those, in particular, who came from the Highlands and Islands.

At some point after resigning from the Partick Burgh Police on May 10, 1909, he returned to Applecross. Renovations on the family home in Culduie were taking place with the addition of an upper storey and the replacement of the heather thatch with slates. It is probable that Kenneth assisted the mason, John Macaulay, until the work was finished.

One anecdote from this time concerns his first communion in the church in Camusterrach. In what would have been undoubtedly a solemn occasion, Kenneth was so overawed by the whole occasion that he put the bread in his pocket rather than partake of the Lord's Supper![4]

The autumn of 1910, however, saw him once again back in Glasgow. And so, with his parents blessing, and the backing of references from Rev. Mr MacIver, now in Glenurquhart, the Rev. D.F. Macleod, Gardner Street, and the Rev. Alex Murray, Applecross, he joined seventy-eight other full-time students at the Bible Training Institute in Bothwell Street.

BTI was noted for its inter-denominational and cosmopolitan flavour, although it attracted most support from students who had a United Free or Baptist background. Now beginning its nineteenth session, the stated aim of BTI was:

> "to give young men and women who offer for missionary service a thorough grounding in the knowledge and use of the English Bible, and in the distinctive doctrines of the Christian faith, as shall, together with a sound practical training, fit them for efficient service in any sphere to which they may be called."[5]

The Institute was not a "rival to the Divinity Halls" but existed to make its students competent in relating the Gospel to "the 'common people' who form the great bulk of the population in every land."[6]

An excerpt from the Bible Institute Report for session 1910-11 will give some idea of the practical work undertaken by the students:

> "During the past session 2,647 meetings, with an aggregate attendance of 250,731, were conducted by the students. These services embraced every variety of work carried on in connection with Church or Missionary organisations, and included Gospel Meetings in Churches, Mission Halls, Lodging Houses, and Factories; Mothers' Meetings, Bible Classes, and Children's Services. A special and most important department of the work that has been fruitful in blessing is the large Bible Classes in Barlinnie Prison for men, and in Duke Street Prison for women, conducted by arrangement with H.M. Commissioners of Prisons, and with the approval and co-operation of the Governors and Chaplains. Our students also undertake work at the public courts, prison-gate, and in the slum districts. Many of them also receive a practical training at the medical dispensaries in the city that will prove invaluable in their subsequent career."[7]

Under the auspices of the Glasgow United Evangelistic Association, students were involved in both the Tent Hall in the Saltmarket and Bethany Hall in Bridgeton. The Annual Report for 1910 of the GUEA describes the work associated with the Tent Hall as follows:

Bible Training Institute, Glasgow, 1911–1912.

Missionary in Lewis, 1913.

13

"The Hall is situated in one of the neediest districts of the city, and by open-air and indoor services, visitation, and other methods, both ameliorative and evangelistic, wonderful work has been done during the past year. Meetings in lodging-houses and kitchens, following up the people by visitation in their home, practical assistance in the securing of employment, and the lending of a helping hand in cases of distress - all these means have been greatly blessed in many instances. The Sabbath Morning Free Breakfast, the Men's Own Meeting on a Sabbath afternoon, Evangelistic and Gospel Temperance Meetings, the Poor Children's Sabbath Dinner, Band of Hope Meetings, the Poor Lads' and Girls' Help, and various other agencies for the welfare of both old and young, have their home in the Tent Hall."[8] It was ascertained that more than 9,500 people on average passed through the doors each week.

The course which Kenneth took at BTI comprised two sessions of ten months each. Not only were the expected biblical, doctrinal, homilectical, evidential, and practical aspects of the Christian faith covered, but also options such as medical and surgical lectures, English grammar and composition, elocution, elementary Latin, and mathematics. Fees were set at £25 per session with short holidays at Christmas and Easter. On completion of the course, a diploma was awarded provided the student "gave satisfactory evidence of Christian character, consecration, and fitness."[9]

Prayer permeated BTI life. It undergirded both the studies and every expression of evangelistic and practical outreach. Scheduled prayer meetings in Bothwell Street took place at noon each Monday and Wednesday to pray for missionaries, evangelists, staff and students. Additional meetings were organised, too, as the need arose. For instance, in connection with the Glasgow Convention for the Deepening of Spiritual Life in October 1911, early morning prayer meetings were held in the Institute. This priority given to prayer was to leave an indelible mark on the young Kenneth Gillies.

In September 1911, the Highlands and Islands Committee of the United Free Church received applications from Kenneth and two other Gaelic-speaking students for financial help to complete their studies at BTI.[10] After due consideration of "the encouraging reports" on them, the following month's recommendation was that not only should they be assisted by a grant but "that their services be utilised for week-end pulpit supply as far as possible."[11] Subsequently, Kenneth spent some time in early 1912 on missionary service in Morvern with the Rev. Alex. MacDiarmid, later to be U.F. minister in Applecross.

Having finished his studies in June of that year, Kenneth went as a lay missionary of the United Free Church of Scotland to the island of Lewis. Serving principally in the communities of Shawbost and Back, it was here that his life-long love affair with the island and its people really began. A place today where he is still remembered with deep affection.

"Many are the stories told of his concern for souls and his faithful efforts to win them for Christ. He cycled miles in all weathers to help the needy. Seeing him one day on the way to visit a sick person, a woman beckoned to her friend, 'Come and see love on a bicycle!'"[12] It was the young missionary's love for people and his desire that they might come to know Christ which left a lasting impression. An impression which was to be left on a much wider company in the years to follow.

After Lewis, he was a missionary for a time in Uig, Skye, assisting the Rev. John MacDougall. Here, too, his memory lives on. One story, however, suggests that Kenneth had a bit to learn in the area of personal etiquette. Lodging in Elgol with the parents of Donald John MacKinnon, later to be minister in Staffin for over twenty years, Kenneth was all dressed up ready to go out when he noticed that his shoes were rather dirty. Without a moment's hesitation he pulled out from his jacket pocket a newly-pressed yellow handkerchief, spat on it, and used it to wipe them clean. The hanky was then promptly put back in place!

Another sphere of service, nevertheless, was to call him from his missionary endeavours and on June 28, 1917, he enlisted in the Royal Navy. What was to follow was to leave its own distinctive hallmark.

With his brother Roddy in the Royal Navy, 1917.

H.M. Mercantile Auxiliary 'Louvain' leaving from a Maltese harbour. (Photograph courtesy of the Imperial War Museum, London).

Chapter 3

Naval Service and Aberdeen Studies

Kenneth served as an Able Seaman for the next two years in the Mediterranean and Black Sea areas. Keen to keep in touch with those back home, he was aware of the strict orders not to give any indication as to where he was in case this information fell into the wrong hands. Nonetheless, by his use (or misuse) of certain biblical texts he was able to get round this injunction. And so, 'I'm presently at the end of Acts 20:15,' rather than just stating where he'd reached in his daily Scripture reading, actually pointed to his being on Malta! His coded messages continued until one of his superiors detected the ploy and put an end to it!

Seven months after joining up, Kenneth was to experience the hand of providence in a miraculous escape from a watery grave. On January 20, 1918, the armed boarding steamer *Louvain*, under the captaincy of Lieutenant-Commander M. G. Easton, was on patrol in the Kelov Strait, near Malta, when it was torpedoed amidships by a German U-boat. It was the dead of night and Kenneth, who had earlier gone up on the top deck to get away from the crowded quarters down below, witnessed the chaos which ensued. The ship went down rapidly, stern first. Men desperately sought to lower the lifeboats but in the confusion and darkness only one raft made it successfully. Observing the futility of the situation, Kenneth headed for the bow of the *Louvain* and was one of the last on deck. As the bow tilted upwards he leapt into the sea where "down, down, down he went, tossed in the water like a leaf owing to the suction of the doomed ship."[1] A non-swimmer, Kenneth thought his end had come.[2]

Later, he was to recount that whilst in the water his thoughts turned to those at home especially picturing his mother's sorrowful reaction to hearing the news of his death. The Sankey hymn *Down in the valley with my Saviour I will go* had been with him the whole day and now, as he began to lose consciousness in the turbulent water, it brought a measure of comfort and assurance.[3]

Some time afterwards, however, he came to amongst a mass of flotsam. Suddenly aware of his situation, he reached out towards a large table-top floating nearby. Hauling himself onto his new-found raft, he clung on until the destroyer *H.M.S. Thesus*, on the look out for survivors, picked him up.

Put ashore at Italy, Kenneth spent some time in hospital recuperating from his ordeal, although a lasting consequence was an habitual cough. Coincidentally during his convalescence, one of his fellow-patients was a relative of his from Little Loch Broom called Kenneth MacGregor who, on finding out that his Applecross cousin's main personal regret through the whole episode was the loss of his Gaelic Bible, graciously gave over his own copy.

A further incident from Kenneth's time in the navy which bears telling was when he had all his teeth removed without anaesthetic! Enough to bring tears to the eyes of the strongest sailor!

The war over, Kenneth found himself towards the end of his term of service in the Black Sea port of Batoum. It was here, whilst awaiting their respective discharge papers, that he met a Cameron Highlander from North Uist, Archie Robertson. Archie recalls their meeting in the early summer of 1919 as follows.

"I shall always remember this place because of meeting a godly young man who was a sailor on a man-of-war stationed there at the time. It was so refreshing to meet one that I could have fellowship with and that in the Gaelic language. I was truly starving for such fellowship, I might say, since I had left home at the beginning of 1917. We were together every day while I remained in that port. I was there for one Sabbath and I went with this sailor and another Christian soldier to a local church, or more like a hall, where Russian Christians worshipped in their own tongue. They were Baptists or probably Brethren and well acquainted with the writings of Spurgeon... We were invited to some of their homes and in one home we...prayed in English and they prayed in their own language. How I wished at the time to have known their language so as to have understood their prayers which seemed so earnest. In another home we dined with the family and we noticed that their habit was to stand around the table while asking God's blessing on the mercies.[4]

In spite of the language difficulties, Kenneth and Archie were able to communicate to some extent with their hosts by using verses in their respective Bibles as guideposts. Consequently, they managed to get themselves a meal on one occasion by pointing out Hebrews 13:2 – "Do not forget to entertain strangers."(!)

Discharged in June 1919, Kenneth was approached by the Highlands and Islands Committee of the United Free Church to resume missionary work in Skye.[5] However, he had already decided to prepare himself for the ministry of the United Free Church and so enrolled on a M.A. degree course at Aberdeen University.

For the next three years Kenneth responded positively to the rigours of study. As a candidate for the Ordinary degree, he was required to take five subjects selected from at least three out of four departments, namely, language and literature, mental philosophy, history and law, and science.[6] Two of the subjects were to be studied for two years which in his case meant Celtic and Moral Philosophy.[7]

In the former of these, the student was introduced to a general Scottish History up to 1500 prior to looking at such material as the poems of MacMhaighstir Alasdair and stories from Keating's History of Ireland.[8] The course was taught in Kenneth's second year by John Fraser, the son of a gamekeeper from Glenurquhart, who in 1921 became Professor of Celtic at Jesus College, Oxford.[9]

Most of the small band who opted for Celtic were either preparing for the ministry or the teaching profession. Three of Kenneth's classmates came from Point in Lewis including his old friend from BTI days, John Murray. Alongside him, there was John MacSween, subsequently a headmaster back in his native island before becoming the first Principal of Lews Castle College in 1951. The last of the trio, Donald Campbell, was to go with Kenneth to the United Free College in Aberdeen.[10]

The Celtic connection with the ministry included two further island contemporaries. Firstly, there was Angus Duncan from Scarp, who went on to distinguish himself academically (as did John Murray) by attaining the post-graduate B.D. After many years in the ministry, he became a Cataloguer with the School of Scottish Studies in Edinburgh.[11] Secondly, there was Lachie Macleod from Berneray, who taught for some years in Harris and Skye before entering the ministry, subsequently serving in various island congregations.[12] In 1955 he demitted his charge in Glenurquhart on being appointed Gaelic Evangelist with the Home Board of the General Assembly of the Church of Scotland. Kenneth and he were to maintain a warm and spiritual friendship over the years.

Kenneth made satisfactory progress through his studies although not without a bit of a struggle at times. In session 1920-21, he achieved an eleventh place in the Order of Merit for Moral Philosophy, whilst the following year he came second to John Murray (out of a total of nine students) in Ecclesiastical History. This particular class contained three Aberdonian men, Robert Smith, Richard Robertson, and Arthur Wallace, who were all to join Kenneth at the U. F. College.[13]

Kenneth's academic high point probably occurred in his final year English Ordinary class when he came joint seventeenth along with John MacSween in the Order of Merit (with Great Credit). The low point, on the other hand, seems to have been practical and systematic Zoology which he had to re-sit. Not surprisingly, he was well down the list in this subject.[14]

During his time at University, Kenneth was a student assistant at Torry U.F. Church (1920-21), a place where he is still remembered as a caring preacher who was particularly interested in the church's youth work. His involvement there saw him take an active part in the Christian Endeavour Group and open air meetings. The summer of 1920 also saw him assigned to do two weeks mission work amongst the fisherfolk in Peterhead.

Whenever he could Kenneth attended the Old Aberdeen Mission located in the former Dr. Bell's school on St. Machar Drive. Instituted in 1881, the Mission's founder, Mr. George McKenzie - who was to be superintendent for 63 years - oversaw a work which sought to reach out to the immediate vicinity around Old Aberdeen by way of evangelistic and cottage meetings, district visitation, tract distribution and Sunday School.

Kenneth's association with the Mission coincided with the busiest period in its history. Over seventy workers gathered for their quarterly meeting at the end of 1921 whilst the numbers of children attending the Sunday School were somewhere in the region of 500-600 per week. The annual Sunday School socials between 1921 and 1924 had to be held on two successive Saturdays due to the large number of friends and parents who wanted to come and see the children take part. Likewise, as many as a thousand people would congregate for the Sunday School picnic at places such as Hazlehead and Persley Den.[15]

Attendance at the Mission, however, was to become even more attractive for Kenneth on account of one of the Sunday School teachers, Mary-Helen (Molly) Stephen. A medical student in her early twenties, Molly was introduced to Kenneth by her younger sister, Minnie, also a medical student. The girls' parents, the Rev. and Mrs Alexander Stephen, had served the Lord for many years as missionaries with the American Baptist Mission in Assam, north-east India, the place where Molly had been born in January 1898. It was not long before Molly herself was introducing "this rather shy, silent young man" to them.[16] Her gracious and spiritual nature had already made a deep impression on the Highland heart of the prospective minister.

By the summer of 1922, Kenneth's University studies were at an end. And so, on July 13, in "one of the heaviest graduations in the whole history of the University of Aberdeen", he joined an assortment of some 224 students - arts, medical, law, divinity, science, and commerce - in the Mitchell Hall, Marischal College.[17]

Graduating along with Kenneth, who was a few days short of his thirty-fifth birthday, was John Macdonald, son of the postmaster in Alligin, Torridon. He was to spend a few years as headmaster in Scalpay, Harris, before undertaking theological studies in Glasgow University. After serving as a Church of Scotland minister in Argyll and Easter Ross, he returned to his roots in 1960 and the charge of Lochcarron and Shieldaig from which he retired six years later.

Others who also had the degree of M.A. conferred upon then at this time included two Lewismen, Angus Maclean from Aird and Murdo Macleod from Back, who were both to return to their homeland as teachers, the former succeeding the latter as headmaster at North Tolsta in 1931. Mr Macleod, on his appointment as head at Back Junior Secondary was to remain there until 1943 when he moved to Glasgow to continue his career. A further graduate, Kenneth Mackenzie from Gairloch, also joined them in Lewis, following his appointment to a post at the Nicolson Institute.[18] One Lewis graduate, however, Alexander Macaulay from Breasclete, a man who had won the Military Cross in 1918, spent his teaching career in Fife.

Once the pomp and ceremony of the graduation was over, Kenneth's desire to enter the ministry required that he undertake two sessions of study at the United Free Church College. Known as Christ's College, this building was situated just beyond Holburn Junction at the west end of Union Street.

He undertook a second assistantship during his time at the U.F. College, this time at the High U.F. Church (1922-24). This congregation was one of three different congregations which met in the spacious church building known as the 'Triple Kirks', on the corner of Belmont Street and Schoolhill. In 1907, St Columba's U.F. Church in Dee Street - the erstwhile 'Gaelic Church' - had united with the High on the understanding that Gaelic services be held each week in the new location.[19] During his attachment a Gaelic

Christ's College Students 1924

Back: Francis Alexander (later Hon. Chaplain to the Queen), Richard Robertson,
Alexander Reid (over 30 years in Edinburgh South Morningside), William Soutar, Robert Smith, William Ross (almost 30 years in Pitlochry East).
Front: Kenneth Gillies, Prof. David Cairns, Donald Campbell *(see also notes 10 and 13)*

service was therefore held every Sunday afternoon at 2.30pm. Kenneth's involvement with the congregation was greater, too, as the church was vacant for the first few months he was there until the Rev. John Bain, the Gairloch-born minister, was inducted in May 1923.

As regards his continuing studies, Kenneth acquitted himself well. For example, he attained a mark of 84% in his second-year English Bible exam. So, at the end of his course in March 1924, he received his leaving certificate from the College signed by the Principal, Professor David Cairns, indicating that he had:

> "*completed the course of theological studies prescribed by the Church, and passed all the Statutory Examinations; and that his character and conduct, so far as is known to the Senatus, are suitable to his purpose of entering on the office of the ministry.*"

The following month in Kyle of Lochalsh he was licensed by the Presbytery of Lochcarron. In the presence of the ministers from Aultbea, Ullapool, Plockton and Lochcarron; the Rev. D.T. MacKay, Tiree, the Highland Evangelist; and two elders:

> "a certificate was read from the College Committee that Mr Gillies had satisfied all their requirements. He produced a lecture on 2 Cor. 13:14 and a sermon on Ruth 1:16 and read clearly and vigorously part of the lecture. The presbytery sustained his exercises with approbation and as they knew him so well for so many years, and he had done so much Christian work they did not feel it necessary to examine [him] further in theology...The presbytery unanimously resolved to license him and the Moderator [Rev D.M. McIver, Aultbea] licensed him in the name of the Lord Jesus Christ to preach the Gospel of Christ and exercise his gifts as a probationer for the Holy Ministry in this church and recommended him to the Grace of God in the discharge of all his duties as a preacher of the Gospel. Thereafter the Rev Malcolm Macleod, Lochbroom, addressed suitable counsels to him and commended him to God in prayer."[20] His life's work was now about to begin.

Chapter 4

Gardner Street Introduction

On May 29, 1924, Kenneth was ordained and inducted into Partick Gardner Street United Free Church of Scotland, Glasgow. Situated on the corner of Muirpark Street, the church broods over a street which rises in an almost perpendicular fashion at one end, reminiscent in some respects of the high road out of Applecross. Bounded by sandstone tenement buildings on all sides, the church is found on level ground not far from the main thoroughfare of Dumbarton Road.

Some eighty or so years prior to the date of his induction, however, Partick was just a village of some 2,000 inhabitants.[1] An 1848 description of the area proves an interesting contrast to what it was to become:

"Partick, a beautiful and romantic village, in the parish of Govan, situated on the banks of the classic Kelvin near its junction with the Clyde. It proves a favourite summer resort both from the beauty of the locality and the reputed salubrity of the air."[2]

The mid-19th century saw rapid population growth as people flocked to the city of Glasgow in search of work. In response to this, the Glasgow City Mission began to conduct Gaelic services amongst the immigrant Highlanders in Partick. As early as 1864, a Lewis-born divinity student, Murdo Macaskill, later to succeed Dr. John Kennedy at Dingwall, was engaged in mission work amongst the Gaels here.[3] By 1875, a committee had been set up to oversee the missionary work of John Macleod, a former divinity student, who had been for some time involved with the Mission. Meetings for worship were initially held in St. Mary's Hall, 292 Dumbarton Road, before a move to the new schoolhouse in Douglas Street took place less than six months later.[4] This street, later renamed Purdon Street, is found on the other side of Dumbarton Road, opposite the entrance to Gardner Street.

In 1877, the Free Church Presbytery of Glasgow sanctioned the cause of the Partick Gaelic Mission with the Rev. George Munro, Hillhead Free Church, appointed Moderator of Session. In February of the following year John Macleod left for Canada and George Macleod (formerly minister of Duke Street Free Church) took his place as missionary.[5]

The steadily growing congregation by this time were keen to have their own building and as a first step bought an Iron Church from Kelvinside Free Church for the sum of £200. Ground was purchased in Douglas Street and the structure was relocated from its original site on Scotstown Old Mill Road. In November 1879 the Rev. Thomas MacLaughlan and the Rev. Thomas Lindsay of the Free Church College, Glasgow, conducted the opening services on the new site.[6]

Partick Gardner Street Church of Scotland today.

In February 1886, a feu contract concerning a plot of land in Muirpark was drawn up between the heritable proprietor, John Gardner, a butcher in Partick, and six men acting as trustees for Partick Free Gaelic Church. As a result, the Iron Church was shortly afterwards uprooted once more and transplanted to what the plans in the title deeds refer to as "the intended street to be called Gardner Street."[7]

Two years later, Presbytery granted the request of the congregation to appoint its own elders following the church's raising to a full ministerial charge. Both of these measures suggest that the church was now on an established footing but, as it was, there were difficult times ahead for the congregation. Financial problems bedevilled the running of the church, whilst the consequences of the Declaratory Act in 1892 meant that at least a quarter of the membership left to join the Free Presbyterian Church. The roll which had seen one hundred and fourteen members in April 1889 fell to sixty-five within five years. However, in February 1895, the appointment as missionary of the Kinlochbervie-born divinity student, Alexander Macrae, saw this decline not only halted but reversed. By the beginning of 1898 the number on the roll was back up to one hundred and eleven.[8]

That same year the church became an independent Free Church in its own right with Mr Macrae called as its first minister. At a special congregational meeting held that November urgent consideration was given to the proposal "that the development and usefulness of the congregation are hindered by the want of sufficient and suitable accommodation."[9] Intimation was made, therefore, "that the congregation proceed to the erection of a new church, on the site of the present temporary structure."[10] Interestingly, in the light of subsequent changes to the building's design, the initial plans for new premises included having the halls *underneath* the church and also a Church Officer's house.[11]

Nevertheless, Presbytery declined to sanction the building of a new church on the site and instead suggested that the congregation move to Thornwood. Not surprisingly, this option was greeted unfavourably in Gardner Street.[12] Some months later, in January 1900, the Kirk Session resolved to approach Presbytery again to have this decision overturned.

Significantly, the uniting of the Free Church of Scotland and the United Presbyterian Church that same year - an initiative with which the Gardner Street people seemingly concurred without much dissent - gave impetus to the vision for a new building. Presbytery now gave its backing to the congregation of the renamed Partick Gaelic United Free Church and their need for more suitable and substantial accommodation.

Nonetheless, there were still a fair number of people who were unsure about whether building a new church was really the right course of action. After all, the financial commitment would be great.[13] At the close of one congregational meeting, several folk stood outside discussing the matter until the Clerk to the Deacons' Court, Donald John Maclennan, a Harrisman, took a piece of chalk from his pocket and wrote on a large stone the words 'Go forward'. Evidently reassured by this demonstration of faith, the assembled

*The 1905 Bazaar Guidebook includes this artist's impression of
Partick Gaelic Church, Gardner Street, as it was intended to be.
It provides an interesting contrast to the photograph on page 24.*

group decided that to venture onwards was the only option.[14] Consequently, by the middle of 1901 streamlined plans had been drawn up at an estimated cost of £3,500.[15]

By the summer of 1902 the new halls were ready but it was to be a further two years, September 24, 1904, before the Memorial Stone of the church building itself was laid. In the interim, the Rev. Alexander Macrae had accepted a call to Creich in his native Sutherland and had left in February 1903. A few months later, a Lewisman, the Rev. Donald F. Macleod, who had previously been in Greenock Gaelic and Avoch, became the second ministerial incumbent of Partick Gaelic. Change was in the air.

On May 13, 1905, the opening of the new church formally took place with Professor Stalker, Professor of Church History and Christian Ethics at Christ's College, Aberdeen, and the Rev. James Macleod, Knockbain, presiding.[16] Notably, these inaugural services saw the congregation stand to sing during public worship for the first time. In addition, the main Sunday morning service was now to be in English with the Gaelic service shifted to 2 pm. These rearrangements were to prove too much for three of the elders who left for the Free Church.[17]

The following October the church held a three-day bazaar in the Institute of the Fine Arts in Sauchiehall Street to try and raise the £1,700 needed to clear the debt on the new church and halls. In the accompanying publicity, attention was drawn to the fact that £3,163 had already been raised by this Gaelic-speaking, working class congregation.[18] Opened by the Lord Provost of Glasgow, Sir John Ure Primrose, it must have been a great success for two months later the Clerk to the Deacons' Court could say, no doubt with some satisfaction, that the congregation were now "entirely free of debt."[19]

The advent of both a new ministry and new church accommodation were to herald times of spiritual advancement within the congregation. Numbers of those either committing themselves to the Christian faith for the first time or transferring into the membership of the church grew relatively quickly. At the communion time in October 1906, for instance, twenty-four people joined by profession of faith whilst, eighteen months later, a total of forty-one became members. By the end of the decade the membership roll had risen to two hundred and ninety-seven. It was no wonder then that the Kirk Session wanted to "express the desire to place on record their thanks to Almighty God for His goodness to them as a church in times gone by and for all the manifestations of His goodwill and grace towards them in awakening and spreading spiritual life in the church."[20]

The autumn of 1907 had seen the church drop the 'Gaelic' part from its name, apparently without much opposition, and adopt instead the title of Partick Gardner Street U.F. Church. Five years later, however, the proposal to introduce hymns and instrumental music created a much stronger current of feeling. And so, whilst the congregation voted three to one for hymns and two to one for music - a result which the Session earnestly hoped that everybody would "cordially accept"[21] - the introduction of an organ and hymn books towards the end of 1912 precipitated the exodus of some thirty members including another three elders. This separation was to be instrumental in the establishment of

Partick Gardner Street U.F. Church

Ordination & Induction

OF THE

REV. KENNETH GILLIES, M.A.

On THURSDAY, 29th MAY, 1924

AT 7.30 P.M.

Rev. WM. JARDINE, M.C., M.A.
Belhaven U.F. Church, Glasgow, will preside

Rev. RODERICK MACLEOD, M.A.
Deputy Superintendent of Highland Missions, will preach

Partick Highland Free Church in later years.[22]

During the traumatic years of the First World War the numbers joining Gardner Street continued to rise and by 1918 the membership had passed the four hundred mark. The Roll of Honour records over one hundred and sixty men associated with the congregation who saw service during this time, twenty-four of whom made the supreme sacrifice.[23]

Further tragedy was to hit the church on New Year's Day, 1919, when the rigged schooner HMY *Iolaire*, full of returning servicemen en route for the island of Lewis, crashed on to rocks a short distance from Stornoway. Two hundred and five men were lost, one hundred and eighty-one of them from Lewis plus another twelve from Harris. With many of the congregation closely connected with the communities so savagely devastated the sense of grief was acutely felt. Deeply affected himself, the Rev. Mr Macleod clearly spoke for the whole church when he described the tragedy as "an awful calamity ... plunging the island into a house of mourning."[24]

By way of practical aid a considerable amount of money was raised by the congregation over the next two years to help those families who were so sorely bereaved. This generosity of spirit was also seen following the severe storms of March 1921 which caused great destruction to manses and churches in the Highlands and Islands.

Around this time, too, Mr Macleod also sought to stimulate the congregation to give monies towards the purchase of a manse. To this end he set up a fund where he offered to match pound for pound - up to the sum of £600 - any money which the congregation could raise. A bold step! In connection with this, the proceeds of a Sale of Work in December 1921 amounted to £218.

Sadly, however, Mr Macleod was to die before sufficient funds could be acquired to buy a manse. In November 1923 the Deacons' Court recorded its appreciation of his ministry as follows:

> "Mr Macleod carried on a devoted and successful ministry in Partick for over twenty years. During that long period he made full use of his many gifts as a pastor and preacher with faithfulness and patience. He fulfilled all the duties of his office. As a preacher he unfolded the truths of the gospel earnestly and affectionately. He was a source of consolation to the afflicted and a trusted counsellor. He was an eloquent evangelical minister of the gospel of free grace, both in Gaelic and English. Shortly after coming to Partick he faced the laborious task of building a new church and had the great pleasure of seeing it being opened free of debt and he was successful in gathering around him a loyal and devoted congregation who today mourns his loss."[25]

Following in the ministerial footsteps of the Rev. D. F. Macleod, Kenneth Gillies was well aware of the affection and esteem in which his predecessor was held. At his induction, he would also have been reminded of the high expectations placed upon him. Presiding at the service was the Rev. William Jardine, Belhaven U.F., who read the charges, assisted by the Rev. Roderick Macleod, Deputy Superintendent of Highland Missions, who

Social Meeting

in the Church, on Friday, 30th May, 1924

REV. ALEX. MACLEAN, M.A.
Interim Moderator, in the Chair

Tea will be served in the Hall from 7 till 7.45 p.m.

PROGRAMME

PRAISE	-	Psalm C. PRAYER
		CHAIRMAN'S ADDRESS
HYMN	-	Rejoice! the Lord is King - - CHOIR
ADDRESS	-	REV. ARCHD. DAWSON Newton Place U.F. Church, Partick.
SOLO	-	My Prayer - MISS CAMERON
ADDRESS	-	REV. EVAN GRANT St. Columba U.F. Church, Govan.
ADDRESS	-	REV. ALEX. ROBERTSON Baptist Church, Partick.
CHORUS	-	Jerusalem - - CHOIR

PRESENTATION OF PULPIT ROBES
Mrs. KERR will robe the Minister.
The lady will be introduced by Mr. M'ASKILL.

PRESENTATION FROM SABBATH SCHOOL CHILDREN. Mr. TORQUIL MACLEOD

ADDRESS	-	REV. KENNETH GILLIES, M.A.
SOLO	-	The Brighter Day - MISS MACLEAN
ADDRESS	-	REV ANGUS M'IVER Glenurquhart.
ADDRESS	-	MR. D. M'LENNAN Applecross.
ANTHEM		O how amiable are Thy Dwellings CHOIR
ADDRESS	-	REV. W. DAVIDSON Somerville Memorial Church, Glasgow.
ADDRESS	-	MR. ARTHUR WALLACE, M.A. Aberdeen.
SOLO		Lord Whom my inmost Soul adoreth MISS URQUHART

PRESENTATION TO INTERIM MODERATOR
MR. D. GRAY.

Reply - - REV. ALEX. MACLEAN, M.A.

PRESENTATION TO SESSION CLERK
MR. R. BRUCE, M.A.

Reply	-	MR. M. M'ASKILL.
VOTES OF THANKS	-	MR. J. S. RIACH
DOXOLOGY	-	Praise God from Whom all Blessings flow.

BENEDICTION.

Programme for the Social Evening following the induction of the Rev. K. Gillies.

preached. At the following evening's Social Meeting - chaired by the Interim Moderator, the Rev. Alex Maclean, Maryhill, who was later to christen the first of Kenneth's two sons - there was a packed programme which included three soloists, three items by the choir, and no less than ten speeches by various ministers and elders. The occasion must have been especially memorable for the Rev. Angus MacIver, whose gospel message had impacted the young Kenneth Gillies so decisively over a decade and a half previously.

The next day the new minister was formally introduced at the 11am English and 2pm Gaelic services by the Rev. Alexander Murray, his former minister in Applecross, and now of Beauly. The 7pm English service Kenneth took himself.

On the Monday evening after his induction, the Deacons' Court met and "expressed the hope that his coming would not only be a great blessing to himself and to the congregation but also a source of spiritual strength to the cause of Christ."[26] Words which with the advantage of hindsight now appear quite prophetic.

Marriage to Molly, July 10, 1924.

Chapter 5

Of Marriage and Ministry

The Gardner Street congregation to which Kenneth came had a demanding schedule of two English and two Gaelic services on a Sunday. Added to this were three prayer-meetings during the week: Gaelic on a Wednesday and Saturday; English on a Thursday. For both midweek gatherings a sermon was required. This rotation of seven services per week was to remain unchanged until the beginning of the Second World War when the less popular Thursday meeting was suspended indefinitely.

On top of this, the Lord's Supper was celebrated four times a year on the fourth Sabbaths of January, April, June, and October. Each occasion requiring several additional services over the communion weekend.

This heavy workload was eased to some extent by ministerial assistants, usually divinity students. But, in order to devote more of his time to prayer and pastoral matters, Kenneth also soon set about establishing a network of preachers to help him. Before this was to take shape, however, another life-changing adjustment was to be made when just six weeks after his induction he married Molly.

The wedding took place on July 10, 1924, in her home church in Aberdeen, Gilcomston Park Baptist Church. The Rev. Grant Gibb officiated, assisted by the minister of the church where Kenneth had recently finished his student attachment, the Rev. John Bain. The best man was his friend from student days, Arthur Wallace.[1] Sadly, just a week after the wedding, Molly's mother, who had been suffering with cancer for some years, passed away.

On returning to Glasgow, the newly-married couple had to wait until September to receive the keys to the new manse at 17 Beechwood Drive, Jordanhill.[2] The purchase of the house was due in no small part to the initiative and generosity of the late Rev. D.F. Macleod who had personally given £933 at the time of his death.[3] A sum roughly equivalent to £25,000 in today's money.

Kenneth and Molly were soon to start a family with Alexander Kenneth, born on November 17, 1925, and Hector John, on February 25, 1928. The latter was named after the doctor who delivered him, Dr Calder.

Molly, however, did not enjoy the best of health. Having contracted pulmonary tuberculosis whilst a medical student in Aberdeen, she was to endure recurrent bouts of sickness for the rest of her life. Shortly after Hector was born, indeed, her future appeared particularly bleak. At her bedside, Kenneth and his father-in-law, the Rev. A. E. Stephen, sought to lay hold of the grace and sustaining power of the Lord Jesus Christ, earnestly entreating God to spare her life until at least the boys were grown up. In faith they based

Rev. and Mrs. K. Gillies, Alexander and Hector, 1929.

their prayers on the promise of Jesus in Matthew 18:19 that, "if two of you shall agree on earth as touching any thing that they shall ask, it shall be done for them of my Father which is in heaven." Evidently, their petition was heard.

Nevertheless, Molly was to have several prolonged stays in the sanatorium at Bridge of Weir. During these times away from home - almost two years on one occasion - the family would only be reunited every two or three months when Kenneth and the boys were able to make the trip. Her absence from both home and church was keenly felt.

As a consequence, Hannah Grant from Shieldaig was taken on to look after the two small boys and keep house for their father. She was to fill this role for five years until Molly was better able to cope with living at home. Following Hannah's departure, a series of live-in maids assisted Molly in the manse.

As minister of a busy congregation, Kenneth was not highly involved in what nowadays would be called active parenting. As discipline was left to Molly, this meant that her absence often resulted in a state of anarchy as far as the boys were concerned! Both attended the nearby Jordanhill School, a nominal fee-paying establishment, with holiday-times spent largely in Applecross staying either in the old family home in Culduie or with

Kenneth's sister and her husband in the remote hamlet of Ardbain. Their father, of course, in being committed to the work in Gardner Street could only manage short sojourns to his homeland.

By December 1926, the membership of the congregation was recorded as three hundred and sixty-eight. What is perhaps surprising, however, is that of this number around one-third of the surnames are of Lowland origin. A significant minority of names such as Fenwick, Porteous, Stark, and Veitch are therefore found interspersed amongst the expected MacLeods, MacDonalds, and Macraes. Allowing for those Highland and Island women who married Lowland men, it is still an observation which tends to bring into question the traditional view of Gardner Street as having been always a purely Gaelic-speaking or Highland church. It would appear on the surface, anyway, that many people joined the church simply because it was in their locality.

Having said that, clearly a large percentage of the congregation consisted of those who had either come south to find work in Glasgow or were descendants of those who had arrived a generation or two earlier. Many of the men found employment on or around the river Clyde whilst others followed in their minister's footsteps and joined the police. Many of the women connected with Gardner Street were either taken on as domestic servants in the big houses in Kelvinside and the surrounding district or were employed as nurses in one of the many city hospitals.

In 1929 the congregation voted ten to one for church union and thus became Partick Gardner Street Church of Scotland.[4] The first five years of Kenneth's ministry had seen significant growth with over sixty people joining by profession of faith. One of God's instruments in bringing people to faith in Christ during this time was the Irish evangelist, W. P. Nicolson, who had made a distinct impression on Kenneth at rallies in the Tent Hall. In later years, W. P. liked to tell of the time when he first preached in "brother Gillies' church" and "though roaring like a bull" it appeared to him that many were fast asleep in the pews. Afterwards, he was gratified to be informed that far from being asleep the custom of many in the congregation was to remain in an attitude of prayer whenever evangelistic addresses were being given. Other evangelists, too, such as D. T. MacKay and Tom Paterson also had opportunities to preach or conduct missions in the church.

Throughout the 1930's the church continued to see a steady stream of new converts with over two hundred joining the church during the decade. This was testimony in no small measure to Kenneth's strongly evangelical preaching based on a solid exposition of the Word. Coupled to this was an earnest sincerity and warm friendship as he went among his people. It was a combination which struck a chord with many. Nonetheless, his consistent emphasis on the love of God for sinners was occasionally criticised by those who thought his approach tended to play down hell and the wrath of God.

Kenneth was a diligent pastor who visited his people faithfully. He was concerned, too, not only for their spiritual state but also their practical needs. Roddy MacKay, one of his future elders, recalls the Sunday evening in 1938 when he first made acquaintance with the Gardner Street minister. Having already been asked as to whether or not he had somewhere to stay, he was more than surprised when Kenneth offered to meet him at his lodgings the next morning to go with him to look for work - a search which was to prove successful. Many a person could testify to finding not only employment but a place to stay through contact with the Rev. Kenneth Gillies.

He firmly believed that faith was to be expressed in action. An oft-repeated Gaelic saying of his summed up this attitude: *Cuiridh Gràdh thu do'n chiste-mhine chum cabhair a nochdadh do'n bhochd. Cuiridh E. thu do'n bharaille-sgadain agus do shlochd a'bhuntàta.* (Love will send you to the meal chest to help the needy. It will send you to the herring barrel and the potato pit.) Unspoken acts of kindness and generosity followed him around as he pastored those in his care.

In the pulpit he displayed the expected saintly solemnity. However, anyone who remotely knew him was soon aware of his big hearty laugh and reputation for playing practical jokes on the unsuspecting. On April Fools' Day one year, for example, he had a letter sent to Molly, supposedly from a firm of solicitors, asking her to call to discuss a legacy which had been left to her by a distant relative in South Africa. Completely believing the contents, she was just on the point of leaving the manse when her laughing husband revealed the truth! There were many who suffered a similar fate over the years.

In getting around the city, Kenneth relied on his feet, his bicycle, and public transport. Later, there were a variety of chauffeurs to drive him - some voluntary, others conscripted! He did try to learn to drive but was put off following an incident in the late 1920's when visiting his Applecross-born friend, the Rev. John Mackenzie, then student assistant in the High U. F. Church in Aberdeen. On a trip up Deeside, Kenneth's attempt at taking the wheel of the car came to an abrupt halt when he drove off the road near Aboyne, collided with a fence, and came to rest in a field! Although the farmer was sympathetic and the occupants unscathed, he never drove again!

Increasingly, there were requests for him to spend communion weekends away from Gardner Street. He especially enjoyed those forays which took him up north and west to minister in various Highland and Island congregations. Sometimes, however, these trips were not without their hazards. During the mid-1930's, for instance, his journey to assist the aforementioned John Mackenzie, who by this time was minister at Strathy on the north coast of Sutherland, was delayed when the bus he was travelling in got stuck in a snowdrift at remote Inchkinloch, some eleven miles south of Tongue, at the south end of Loch Loyal.

Providentially, a solitary house nearby was occupied by a shepherd, Samuel MacDonald, and his wife, Kate. Trooping off the bus, the stranded passengers and driver were delighted to discover that the shepherd's wife had been busy that day doing a larger-than-usual baking! Furthermore, it turned out that she just happened to be a second cousin of Kenneth's! He seemed to always bump into someone just when he needed to!

At the outbreak of World War Two, Molly and the boys were evacuated from Glasgow to Kilmarnock where her sister, Minnie, lived. Remaining behind to see to his congregation, Kenneth also trained as an air-raid warden. Around this time, too, he became chaplain to the Royal Beatson (Cancer) Hospital. This was a place which several of his ministerial colleagues had difficulty visiting on account of the malodorous effects of some of the treatments. It was to be the start of a mutually-enriching relationship between patients, staff, and chaplain, spanning the next three and a half decades.

A pre-war photo of the Beechwood Manse.

Eighteen months after war broke out, and with the whole family together once more in the Beechwood manse, the Clydeside Blitz began. The night of March 15, 1941, saw German aircraft pass over every three minutes dropping all manner of bombs and incendiary devices. The damage the following morning was immense with the nearest bomb having exploded some two hundred yards away in Eastcote Avenue. The front door of the manse was shattered and several windows had been blown out whilst the ceiling in the washhouse also came down. In Gardner Street, the roof of the church hall sustained damage. Despite this destruction, the family were grateful to be alive as several people known to them were killed in the raid.

The following night in the manse there was, understandably, a state of alarm. Kenneth's reading of Psalm 91 did bring a measure of comfort to the family as everyone, including the maid, huddled together in the cupboard under the stair as the drone of aircraft heralded the resumption of the barrage. The next day, umpteen pieces of shrapnel were retrieved from the garden. Over the following months, further sporadic air-raids were to renew afresh this general atmosphere of fear and tension.

On a lighter note, in the July of that year, Alexander joined his father at the communions in Uig, Skye, where unbeknown to him his future wife was part of the congregation! They stayed with the Rev. Alexander MacKinnon who, on learning that Kenneth was about to preach from the book of Ruth, commented, "Not out with that woman again!" The Gardner Street minister's fondness for this Old Testament text was well known!

During the war years, too, Kenneth would often return from the north and west laden down with eggs, salted mutton, or even a case full of venison. All a very welcome supplement to the restricted rations in the city!

Back in Gardner Street, the inaugural meeting of the Young People's Union in September 1942 saw over thirty young folk present. This was something of a development for a church where little by way of organised events outwith the usual church services took place, apart from the annual Sunday School picnic and the yearly Congregational Meeting. Pre-war there had been a Girls' Brigade, a Woman's Guild, and the regular Sale of Work, but all had ground to a halt with Molly's illness. Consequently, there were murmurings within the congregation as to the need for any kind of youthwork at all but Roddy MacDonald, the minister's assistant and prime mover for the group, had the full support of both Kenneth and his wife.

Varied in character, there were debates on topical issues, talks from missionaries and members of the caring professions, games, and cycle rambles. Sometimes, the youth from Partick Congregational Church attended. Controversy arose on one occasion following the showing of three films brought along by the Rev. Kenneth Stewart, Port of Glasgow chaplain. Innocuous enough by today's standards, one film was on the merchant navy, the second on the British Sailors' society, and a third entitled 'Peter and Andrew'. The reaction of some of the elders in the eyes of the young people was predictably unfavourable.

January 1944 saw the Rev. Duncan Campbell, then United Free Church minister in Falkirk, visit Gardner Street. He made an immediate impact on many including Kenneth's son, Alexander, who wrote in his diary, "Communion - great minister! The fiercest I have ever heard, I think. Struck the pulpit, clapped his hands and shouted. He was great and evangelistical!"

The following October, Duncan Campbell returned for a week of meetings which were characterised by a strong sense of the presence of God. Many were moved and several converted. Later to be so significantly involved in the Lewis Revival, his relationship with Kenneth Gillies and the Gardner Street congregation was to be long-lasting and fruitful.

On Thursday, February 17, 1944, the congregation met to celebrate their minister's twentieth year in Gardner Street. Kenneth was given a generous cheque for £92 10/- (a

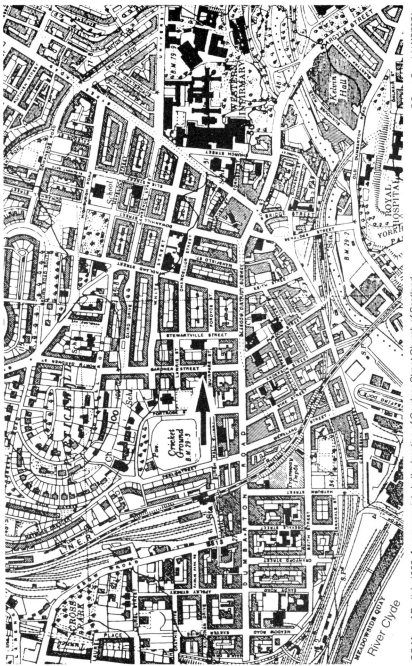

OS Map of Partick, 1938. An arrow points to the location of Gardner Street Church of Scotland.

sum around £1,700 today) whilst Molly received a handbag with £30 inside. It was a clear indication of the gratitude and love that the people had for their pastor and his wife.

By the time the war finished, however, Molly's life was slipping away. Days on end were spent in bed as fever and sickness took their grip. Eventually, she passed into glory on January 4, 1946, just a few days short of her 48th birthday. After a memorial service in Gardner Street, her remains were taken by train and boat to Applecross for burial. Alexander, who was with the Royal Signals in India, did not receive word of his mother's death until nine days later.

A mother of two young men who were a credit to her, she was also a friend and counsellor to many in the church. Her presence and wisdom are still remembered with affection. One piece of advice she gave to one prospective minister was, "Whatever you do, don't have either a Highlander or a banker as your church treasurer!" Obviously borne out of some frustrating experiences! A pillar of support to Kenneth, she had taken her place with dignity and grace at her husband's side, actively and prayerfully involved in the life and mission of the church when her illness allowed. Kenneth missed her greatly although like many Highland men found it difficult to communicate his thoughts and feelings to his sons. After twenty-one years of marriage and ministry it was a painful separation.[5]

Chapter 6

Days of Grace and Glory

After twenty or so years in the ministry, Kenneth's web of influence meant he was frequently up on the movements of those he could call upon to take services. It has to be said, however, that sometimes his methods of getting them into the pulpit were morally questionable! For instance, many a minister of the gospel found themselves in the position where they were expected to preach in Gardner Street only after seeing their name under the church notices in the Saturday edition of the *Evening Citizen*! Even returning on leave from the forces, as the Rev. Roddy MacDonald discovered, did not mean exemption from this particular form of contact.

In his case, he had arrived back in Glasgow from France in the early hours of a Sunday morning, having travelled for the most part by train. It had been an exhausting journey and, as he wearily made his way to his uncle's home in Caird Drive, he could think of little else but falling straight into bed.

Quietly entering the house, he made his way into the kitchen where he noticed a glass of milk left out for him. However, what really caught his attention was a copy of the paper, propped up against the tumbler and open at the relevant page, announcing his impending appearance in Gardner Street a few hours later!

After having this kind of treatment dished out to him a few times, it was no wonder that he decided to get his own back. Enlisting the help of his friend, John Macleod (Arnol),[1] who had also suffered similar treatment at the hands of Kenneth Gillies, they hatched a plan to catch out the Gardner Street minister.

So, appearing unannounced one Sunday afternoon for the Gaelic service, they were well aware that if things went to form then they would be most likely pounced upon to take the evening meetings. Sure enough, at the end of the service, Kenneth took them to one side where he proceeded to inform them that John would be taking the English service and Roddy the Gaelic after-meeting.

Already prepared for this proposal, Roddy made a light-hearted show of objecting on the grounds that as a former assistant he should get priority and do the English service. Both of them, however, had already made up their minds that whatever arrangement was made neither of then would appear in either pulpit - and neither they did! Kenneth was therefore left to take both evening services! The next time they met him, he gave them something of a chiding but, to quote Roddy, "in a friendly way."

Some ministers tried less direct ways to avoid being put upon at such short notice. The Rev. Murdo Macleod, Tarbert, arrived one evening at the English service and sat in the back seat with a scarf wrapped round his neck to hide his ministerial collar. It didn't work!

Spotted by one of the elders, the news was relayed to Kenneth who, during the intimations, declared that Mr Macleod would be taking the Gaelic after-meeting! Many could testify to being treated similarly.

Kenneth expected those called to the ministry to be prepared to preach at any time. Having said that, he sought to give encouragement and support wherever he could and, in particular, to those who were training for the ministry. The Rev. Donald Macrae, Tarbert, on the occasion that he had to preach in front of his tutor, A. J. Gossip, the Professor of Practical Theology, remembers the helpful advice he received from Kenneth Gillies.

"There will be a big congregation that evening so never mind where the Prof. will be - he's a small man, anyway! Fire away with Highland fervour, speak slowly and audibly, use gestures with your arms if you want, and keep your voice raised, for he's an old man and inclined to be deaf!"

Afterwards, what impressed the somewhat deflated Mr Macrae was that Kenneth accompanied him and his professor to the bus-stop on Dumbarton Road, rather than rush off to take the Gaelic service. In seeking to uplift the young preacher, Kenneth Gillies once again demonstrated that he had time for people.

Following his wife's death, Kenneth busied himself in the demands of his work within the city. Moreover, invitations to various communions in the Highlands and Islands continued unabated. He was also asked to help out with vacant Gaelic-speaking charges from time to time and in March 1948 spent a month in Kilmuir, Skye.

These regular absences from Glasgow led to a somewhat tongue-in-cheek presentation the following year to mark his 25th Anniversary in Gardner Street, when he was given not only the generous sum of £140 but a strong suitcase to assist with his travels north and west! Seven ministers spoke that evening including the Very Rev. Alex Macdonald, St Columba's, who had been Moderator of the General Assembly the previous year.

Of course, when not away on one of his sojourns, Kenneth was still very much out and about amongst his people in the city. He was such a familiar sight striding down the likes of Crow Road that he was often able to flag down trams or buses between stops! Sometimes, too, he would get a free ride to wherever he was going. This was particularly the case if the conductor mistook him for a priest - something which gave him some amusement! One problem he did have with public transport, however, was the number of umbrellas he left on board. Consequently, he was a frequent visitor to the Glasgow Corporation Lost Property department!

The dawn of the 1950's saw no letting up of Kenneth's workload with visiting the housebound and those in hospital high on his list of priorities. In these situations, his comforting prayers and gracious presence were often felt to be as therapeutic as any medical treatment. Funerals, too, saw his sureness of touch as he spoke and prayed with deliberate dignity and poise, bringing comfort and solace to many. As one of his elders recalls, "he was a messenger who brought consolation to a soul that was cast down, a word in season to those who were weary, and balm for those sorely wounded."[2]

Each Sunday, new faces in church were spotted, welcomed, and followed up. Those, too, who'd missed church were similarly noted and followed up! He had an excellent memory for names and was especially interested and adept at connecting people one to the other.

In October 1950, Duncan Campbell held a fortnight's mission in the church which led to several conversions. Preaching at both evening meetings on Communion Sunday, the numbers attending the Gaelic service were so great that the upstairs hall proved too small for the congregation and they had to return to the main sanctuary. Over the next three communion seasons, twenty people joined the church by profession of faith, a number which had not been matched for twenty years.

Duncan Campbell and Kenneth Gillies at a Faith Mission Convention in Stornoway.

This was the time of the Lewis Revival and, not surprisingly, the strong island connections meant that there was a knock-on effect in Gardner Street as the stories of conversions to Christ and the movings of the Spirit were told. It was "a community saturated with God [where] the presence of God was a universal, inescapable fact: at home, in the church, and by the roadside. Many who visited Lewis during this period became vividly conscious of the spiritual atmosphere before they reached the island."[3]

Kenneth's desire during this exciting period was to witness the grace of God at work in people's lives. At the same time, too, he was careful not to over-emphasise or unduly encourage any of the supernatural manifestations which were associated with this move of God's Spirit. Nonetheless, there were amongst his congregation occasional 'faintings' and, more rarely, the sight of individuals going into a trance.

The mutual calling on their ministries saw Kenneth Gillies and Duncan Campbell bound together in the work of the Lord. They frequently spent time together in prayer with half-nights before the throne of grace not uncommon. No wonder their friendship has been likened to that of David and Jonathan! In 1958, Duncan Campbell became Principal of the Faith Mission Training Home and Bible College in Edinburgh, a move which further reinforced the already strong bond between Gardner Street and the work of the Mission.[4] Kenneth's support for the Faith Mission was to prove beneficial to them in those communities in the Western Isles, in particular, who were reluctant to accept the presence of women pilgrims publicly preaching or giving testimony. As he remarked on more than one occasion, "Who am I, or any man, to speak against the work of the grace of God, no matter what instrument God wishes to use."

In the early spring of 1955 Billy Graham came to the Kelvin Hall in Glasgow. His

Partick Gardner Street Church of Scotland.
The noticeboard is promoting an evangelistic rally in the Kelvin Hall
as part of the 1954 'Tell Scotland' Campaign.

campaign was well supported by the Gardner Street congregation with Kenneth both on the organising committee and a counsellor. The young American's evangelistic preaching had such a powerful effect on many of the church's adherents that no fewer than twenty-one of them joined the church by profession of faith at the April communion time. This was to be the highest number of first communicants at any single communion in the fifty-two years of Kenneth's ministry.

During this period, too, Kenneth was actively involved in promoting the work of the Tent Hall through his position as one of the Directors of the Glasgow United Evangelistic

Association. Principally concerned with the Evangelistic and Ameliorative department of the G. U. E. A.'s work, he had been first brought on to the Committee of Management in 1934. His years of prayerful service and support were to leave lasting memories. One former Superintendent of the Hall, Peter Donald, describes him "as having an indefinable sense of the Lord, never moody or resentful, always placid, serene, and consistent."

John Moore, his successor in Steel Street, recalls that, "Mr Gillies was not one to monopolise the conversations and discussions of the Board, but he was always there with the right comment at the right time, and never hesitated to be counted in votes that were important to the evangelical cause." Indeed, he would often ask Kenneth to accompany him on tours in the Highlands and Islands to publicise and generate support for the work.

One Saturday night in the Tent Hall when Kenneth was to be the main speaker, he was joined on the platform by a policeman, Angus MacInnes, who was to give his testimony. He was an accomplished piper who since his conversion had learned to play psalm tunes on his pipes. At first, he was rather unsure as to whether or not this would be acceptable practice at the various city venues he was asked to speak. But, by the time of this meeting, he was able to claim biblical support. Quoting from 1 Kings 1:40, he noted that at the coronation of Solomon, "the people piped with pipes, and rejoiced with great joy, so that the earth rent with the sound of them." He therefore reasoned, "Well, if the ground shook at the playing of the pipes, it *must* have been bagpipes!" Kenneth's response was to laugh heartily and, in typical fashion, lean back and raise his two feet from the floor before letting them down with a thud.

Another time of some amusement at the Tent Hall happened when the visiting preacher called on all those ministers who were in their first charge to stand up for prayer. Many present could not prevent a smile crossing their lips when amongst those standing they saw the minister of Gardner Street - only thirty years into his ministry!

Kenneth loved seeing others being called into the ministry and, in one prayer meeting in 1955, it was to be he who would be the means of confirmation for one young man from Lewis.

During his sermon that night Kenneth paused for a while before mentioning that certain verses were being impressed upon him so much so that he felt he had no option but to read them. Little did he realise the effect this was going to have! As he read the words from Matthew 28, "All power is given unto me in heaven and in earth. Go ye therefore and teach all nation teaching them to observe all things", Kenny (Bàn) MacDonald was hearing not just words but God's call to leave his job and train for the ministry. Earlier that day he had prayed to the Lord that if Mr Gillies, at that evening's meeting, were to quote these words of Jesus then he would go.

Straight after the meeting - and having heard little else in the interim - he went to the vestry and excitedly told his minister everything. Kenneth equally could not contain himself and taking hold of Kenny "like a doll" started swinging him round and round exclaiming, "I knew it! I knew it!"[5]

Glasgow United Evangelistic Association (Evangelistic and Ameliorative Committee) 1959.
Back: T. McGrail (Treasurer), Rev. J.D.B. Robertson (John Street Baptist), A. Dawson, C. Anderson, J. Moore (Tent Hall Supt.), Rev. K. Gillies.
Front: G. Harrison, D. Drysdale, Rev. R.L. Telfer (Springburn Congregational), C. MacFarlane, Dr.J. Kelly (Chairman), J.P. Williamson (Secy.), G. Buckley (Lennoxtown Mission), J. Wybar.

Kenneth always sought to bring encouraging advice to those who desired to preach the Word of God. One Sunday evening, one of the young men in the church was due to preach for the first time. Archie Macleod, however, was rather nervous. Turning to Kenneth in the pulpit he said, "Mr Gillies, please take the reading and opening prayer yourself and I'll do the sermon." "No, Archie," came the reply. "The man that's going to use the scythe must sharpen it himself!" A word of exhortation laced with heavenly wisdom.

The large Highland community in Gardner Street certainly had its fair share of preachers who served them well in both Gaelic and English. Nevertheless, Kenneth's pulpit was never just the preserve of Highlanders. Indeed, his life experience and city location saw him in touch with a wider spectrum of evangelicalism than might have been the case in the Highlands and Islands.

Illustrating this point were preachers such as Brigadier-General Frost O.B.E.; a Czech minister called Karl Kulek; and Professor J.G. Riddell, Professor of Divinity at Glasgow University. This diversity of speakers from different evangelical backgrounds encouraged a wider outlook than may have been expected. Consequently, denominational barriers meant little to Kenneth. Whoever proclaimed the grace and truth of the message of Jesus Christ was welcomed warmly by him.

Various missionary organisations including the Worldwide Evangelistic Crusade (who had a college in Hyndland), the British Syrian Mission, and Hebrew Christian Alliance, all had open invitations to come and address the congregation. This deep-seated interest in mission work at home and abroad was further reflected in Kenneth's personal support and patronage of several societies.

With pulpit supply, of course, there was always the risk that the preacher might not show up. On one Sunday morning when this happened in Gardner Street, however, the only divinity student present had already been primed through a remarkable dream he'd had a few nights earlier. In his dream, he suddenly became aware of the figure of Kenneth Gillies asking him to prepare a sermon for the following Sunday morning, as he would be called upon to preach instead of the expected preacher. Sure enough, as John Murdo Smith sat down in the pew, he was approached by a rather agitated elder who asked him if he could take the service in place of the man who'd failed to turn up. Forewarned, and thus forearmed, he made his way to the pulpit. It has to be said that this was one of the more unusual ways in which Kenneth was involved in getting people to preach![6]

Communion times in the church saw young and old alike exhorted to witness to Christ publicly. Never a season passed without Kenneth stressing from the Word of God the importance of individuals confessing with their mouths the Lord Jesus. All who believed in their hearts that God had raised Christ from the dead were encouraged to respond in faith to God's offer of salvation. He was always careful to emphasise the priority of the Holy Spirit's work, reflected in the words of Jesus in John 6:44, "No man can come to me, except the Father which hath sent me draw him."

Prayer undergirded Kenneth's life and ministry, and was reflected in the attitude of the congregation. A favourite quote of his was, "No prayer, no blessing! Little prayer, little blessing! Much prayer, much blessing!" He prayed in church; in the manse; in cars; in hospitals; on pavements; in homes - wherever he could. It was not uncommon for him to return home at one or two o'clock in the morning after a spontaneous prayer-time in someone's house. Many drew strength, comfort, and joy from his prayer language which, in its grasp of Scripture, revealed something of his relationship with God.

Frequently, he would open meetings with a prayer which incorporated the opening verse of the hymn by William Pennefather, "Jesus, stand among us in thy risen power, let this time of worship be a hallowed hour."[7] Another favourite phrase he used in his approach to God was, "Whose we are and whom we serve." Mirroring the priority he gave to prayer, one of his best-loved spiritual songs was *Don't stop praying.*[8]

> *Don't stop praying! the Lord is nigh;*
> *Don't stop praying! He'll hear your cry;*
> *God has promised, and He is true:*
> *Don't stop praying! He'll answer you.*
>
> *Don't stop praying, but have more trust;*
> *Don't stop praying! for pray we must;*
> *Faith will banish a mount of care:*
> *Don't stop praying! God answers prayer.*

This was a chorus which went back to his times at BTI. Half a century on, he and his student-friend from these days, Willie Meikle (for a number of years pastor of Dumbarton Baptist Church), would still sing it during the times they'd meet up in the Beechwood manse. In Gardner Street house meetings, too, it was a firm favourite.

Kenneth truly was a man of prayer who delighted in communing with his Lord, interceding on behalf of others, and leading his people to the throne of grace. He believed with all his heart that the "effectual fervent prayer of a righteous man availeth much" (James 5:16), and was convinced that the union of believers in prayer has the promise of the "dew of heaven". Undoubtedly, it was through prayer that Kenneth Gillies was given the necessary spiritual resources to equip him for his ministry.

Chapter 7

The Miles Mount Up

Each year, Kenneth made a point of going to the Keswick Convention, a gathering where he invariably enjoyed much Christian uplift and fellowship. It was also one of the few places where he went around without his ministerial collar. It was noted, however, that he never did really master the art of knotting his tie!

One time there, he met up with a group of nurses from Gardner Street on their day off. Standing outside a tea-room whilst he was inside paying the bill, the girls overheard some ministers nearby remarking how "Highland" Kenneth Gillies was. What they then made of this seventy-year old strolling out to rejoin his entourage of young ladies one can only imagine!

Kenneth also regularly attended the annual Strathpeffer Convention. Here, in this relaxing atmosphere, his sense of humour often found unsuspecting victims. Enjoying a siesta one afternoon in the hotel that they were both staying in, the Rev. Neil MacInnes, Glenshiel, was awakened by the sound of uproarious laughter in the lounge from those who'd been summoned by Kenneth's call of, "Come and see this!" What they then saw was the sight of the minister's trailing hand draped over the arm of the chair and just above a strategically placed beer bottle!

Ministers dared not fall asleep anywhere in Kenneth's vicinity. Returning from Lewis on board the *Loch Seaforth*, a certain Free Church man was stretched out having forty winks. On waking, he found his shoelaces had been tied together! Impish pranks followed in Kenneth Gillies' wake.

These many trips away from Glasgow, particularly to the Highlands and Islands, led to several wry observations on his journeying. At a Congregational Meeting in Gardner Street, the Rev. Angus MacKinnon, St Columba's, noted that, "Mr Gillies just lives a penny ha'penny tram ride away from my manse and I never see him. But anytime I am in Kyle of Lochalsh I meet him!"

During a Gardner Street prayer-meeting, too, this impression was voiced by one of the elders, Kenneth Morrison, who was heard to pray, "Lord, bless and protect our minister when he is here with us; and also when he is away - for he is gone so often." A prayer which resulted in the sound of stifled chuckling behind the lectern!

On March 21, 1958, Kenneth assisted at the marriage of his son, Alexander, to Margaret Buchanan, a nursing sister from Skye. Alexander's subsequent appointment as the doctor on Flotta, one of the Orkney Islands, opened up new territory for his father to go and preach. It also served as a location for what was really his only leisure pursuit, fishing.

Alexander and Margaret's Wedding Day, March 1958.
Back: Rev. M. MacSween, Babs Ferguson (bride's cousin), 'Groom and Bride',
Hector, Dona Nicolson (bride's niece), Rev. K. Gillies.
Front: Miss E. Stephen (groom's aunt), Mrs. C. Buchanan (bride's step-mother).

This was an activity which Kenneth thoroughly enjoyed especially if the mackerel were plentiful and taking the feathered lures on the hand-line two or three at a time. Right up to the year before he died, he would jump at opportunities to go out on the sea.

However, returning from an evening's fishing out from Culduie in 1960, he found he literally had to jump *from* it! The tide had ebbed so much that the boat ground to a halt in the mud far down the shore. Undaunted by this, Kenneth picked up an oar and, standing on the gunwale of the boat, placed one end in the mud and vaulted across to more secure ground. Not bad for someone in their 74th year who had just become a grandfather.

Some months after his first grandson's arrival, Kenneth lost one of his dearest friends with the death at the age of fifty-one of the Rev. Murdo MacSween, minister of Govanhill Church of Scotland. They had been closely involved in the Lord's service ever since Murdo had been an assistant in Gardner Street almost thirty years previously. Indeed, it was he who had officiated at Alexander's wedding just over two years previously.

The evening of his passing saw Kenneth call on Mrs MacSween and her three children. As on many a sad visit to a house in mourning, Kenneth's genuine compassion was witnessed as he sought to bring expressions of consolation and comfort. As an example of his care for bereaved souls the following letter reflects something of his pastoral touch.

Dear Miss M_____

I was very sorry to learn that you have been overtaken by a fresh sorrow. My sympathy goes out to you at such a time. Still may the hours of sorrow be hallowed by a more real sense of the nearness of God's presence. The knowledge that He is over all enables us to bow in submission, and may you not sorrow as others which have no hope but realise that for your loved one it is indeed a blessed happiness now to look upon the face of Him whom she loved to serve, and to join those who have gone before in their eternal service and praise. May your heart be stayed upon Jehovah.

> *Yours in sympathy*
> *K. Gillies*

His former elder, Donald John Smith, describes him thus. "As a pastor, he was the real man helpful in all situations. As a preacher, he was simple and to the point just what the average church person needs."[1]

Two main aims influenced his preaching. Firstly, to convict the unconverted of their sins and, secondly, to lead them to a saving knowledge of Jesus Christ as Saviour and Lord. The Rev. John Ferguson, in his memorial tribute, captures well the essence of Kenneth Gillies' preaching.[2]

"In the pulpit, Mr Gillies had a unique style. The delivery was slow and precise, and if lacking the animation characteristic of the Celtic spirit, the preacher's sincerity never failed to impress. Sometimes when gripped by the urgency of his message, a large hand would come into action. The subject matter of his sermons, in English and Gaelic, was always easy to grasp, with the themes invariably converging on the plenitude of the glorified Lord for man's present and future needs. Rarely in his preaching was any reference made to his own experiences, and although an occasional illustration was used, his wide knowledge of Scripture was his main source for elucidation."

It was not eloquence in the pulpit which primarily endeared him to so many but rather his presence amongst his people. The warm handshake, the mingling with the worshippers, the care and generosity of spirit all served to inspire devotion. In his pastoral duties he unstintingly strode up and down streets, climbing countless flights of tenement stairs. Towards the end of his life, he liked to reckon that all told he had walked as many miles as to the moon and back!

Increasingly, too, the congregation was becoming more and more dispersed as people moved away from the immediate Partick area to live in the suburbs and new towns around about Glasgow. Some, obviously, transferred to local churches but many maintained their ties with Gardner Street. Consequently, the geographical sphere of his pastorate was growing more widespread.

He also sometimes found himself in scenarios which were atypical of a Highland

Presbyterian minister. For instance, in visiting Rotten Row Maternity Hospital to see those mothers and their babies who were connected with the congregation, he would make a point of finding out if there were any others from the Western Isles. Regularly, he would come across mothers from the Southern Isles of Barra and South Uist who, despite being of a different religious persuasion, were delighted to converse with someone who was able to speak to them in Gaelic.

Another situation arose when a Pakistani family became next-door neighbours. Shortly afterwards, an invitation to come in for a cup of tea led to some discussion on matters of faith. The sight of the two men sitting down with open copies of the Bible and the Koran before them must have been especially interesting. Sadly, this neighbour was later killed in a road accident on nearby Clarence Drive. Typically, Kenneth was one of the first to visit the sorrowing widow and children and offer comfort.

At Presbytery, although a conscientious attender, Kenneth was neither a committee man nor ambitious. During the latter part of his ministry, he sometimes sat with the Rev. John G. Fraser where they would share asides "perhaps more often when we felt the business was not going in line with or keeping to the standards of the Declaratory Articles in making the Word of God the supreme rule of faith and conduct."[3] Nevertheless, even amongst those ministers in Presbytery who did not share Kenneth's evangelical zeal he had many friends. For his part, he continued to remember them in prayer before the throne of grace seeking that they would be touched by the love of God in Christ and restored to zealous service for Him.

Within Gardner Street, his oversight of the congregation kept happy both those who were more inclined to a traditional Gaelic-speaking emphasis, and those who were more at home in expressing their faith in English. At both Kirk Session and Deacons' Court meetings his subtle charm defused potentially difficult situations. Moreover, he could exercise what one former elder terms "sanctified flyness!" For example, a sum of money was donated to the church to provide individual communion cups. This the Session agreed to act upon. However, the matter subsequently disappears from the minutes and, needless to say, the cups were never bought!

In April 1964, the fortieth anniversary of Kenneth's induction to Gardner Street was celebrated. The Rev. W. F. Grieve, Moderator of Glasgow Presbytery, noted that he had:

> "sustained a most effectual ministry and been the beloved minister, adored
> pastor, and father in God to a great company of people and been instrumental
> in inducing several young men to undertake the service of the Church."[4]

In turn, Kenneth "remarked that it was a joy to be surrounded by a sympathetic people over the years [and] expressed his gratitude to God for His unfailing grace." He then thanked the congregation for the pocket watch and handsome donation presented to him by the oldest member, Donald Maclean, a man who had been associated with the church for sixty-eight years. On the same occasion, further satisfaction was gleaned when his son, Hector, was dedicated as a Lay Reader by Presbytery.

Down through the years of his ministry there were always several policemen who worshipped in Gardner Street, some serving the Lord as office-bearers in the church. Kenneth kept to the forefront his links with the police either by visiting the Training School to meet and address new recruits or through his presence as a speaker at Christian Police Association Meetings. The rapport and mutual affection that he enjoyed with the Glasgow City Police often meant that police cars would stop and offer him a lift when they passed him on the street!

His police connections, too, managed to save the skin of one of the members in his congregation. Leaving a prayer-meeting one evening in Donald Livingstone's trusty old Morris, Kenneth and he were so engrossed in conversation that inadvertently they jumped a red light at the top of Crow Road and were flagged down by a police officer. However, on approaching the car and noticing the minister in the passenger seat, he exclaimed, "Oh! It's yourself, Mr Gillies!" Kenneth replied, "It is indeed, constable. I'm afraid we were talking and never noticed the lights. I'm sure Mr Livingstone will never do it again." A short while later the constable bade farewell to the minister before turning to the driver and admonishing him with a stern, "See and don't do that again!"

By the 1960's, Kenneth had conducted so many weddings that they now included several individuals whose parents he'd married a generation back! Mostly, these were

He always sought to meet people on their level.

53

With grandson Donald in Tongue, 1964.

happy occasions which passed off without a hitch. One time, however, the hour was fast approaching for the marriage service to begin but there was no sign of the Gardner Street minister. Anxiously, the church officer, Donald John Smith, began to scour the neighbourhood and eventually spotted him crossing Dumbarton Road. After quickly telling him about the wedding party awaiting him in the church, Kenneth checked his diary to find he'd marked in the wrong date. Swiftly making his way towards Gardner Street, he entered the vestry, put on his robes, and emerged into the sanctuary just in time and completely unruffled!

At the receptions which followed, Kenneth would invariably inject his own brand of innocent humour. One of his favourite stories concerned three middle-aged maids who were overheard discussing the qualities they were looking for in a man. The first one said, "I would want a man of learning, culture, and well-travelled. Yes! An intellectual." The second announced, "I would like a man of substance, plenty of money, and business acumen." The third, however, stated, "I would like a man of good appearance - and I do hope he appears soon!"

During the mid-1960's a spiritual awakening took place in Gardner Street which resulted in several conversions. Earnest prevailing prayer, sincere and forceful preaching from the likes of Raymond McKeown,[5] and missions such as the one in February 1965, led by Duncan Campbell and assisted by Mary Morrison, were all vehicles for the Lord to use. House-meetings took place for a time each Friday evening at which over thirty people regularly came together to sing, pray, and seek God. Some of those converted at this time went on to become elders in Gardner Street such as Norman Macleod, Calum Iain Morrison, and Kenny Paterson, whilst others included the current minister of Gardner Street, the Rev. Roddy Morrison.

As a result, Kenneth was able to write in his annual Minister's Message in February 1966, "we have seen some of our folk making profession of faith; prodigals have come back home; the faltering have been strengthened and our souls have been built up and confirmed. Once again we desire humbly to acknowledge the blessings and mercies of our Heavenly Father, and to express our grateful thanks for His good hand upon us in all our Church Life."

Arising out of this heightened spirituality came a number of practical initiatives such as the Christmas distribution of food parcels to those in need within the congregation. Another avenue of help followed the visit in early 1969 by the Chinese evangelist, Dr Andrew Gih, when it was agreed to sponsor the adoption of an orphan. Interestingly, the child was given the name Kenneth Gillies![6]

Towards the end of the decade there was renewed concern that young people from the Highlands and Islands were being lost to the church.[7] It was resolved that efforts be redoubled to seek out those who came to the city for work or study, and encourage them to come to a place of worship. In February 1970, writing in *The Gard*, the magazine of the Young People's Group in Gardner Street, Kenneth related the story of what could happen if people took seriously the commission to reach out with the Good News.

"One Sunday evening some time ago there was passing by the door of our Church at service time a lady and her daughter who had not been in church for years and who had little interest in what the Church stands for. But the open door seemed to invite them to enter, and they did enter and were kindly received and shown to a seat. One of our Highland girls watching this spoke to them at the close of the service, and to her they opened their hearts. That young Highland lass went home that night with the lady and her daughter and left them not until they were both rejoicing in the Lord. They made a public profession of their faith in Christ and are now in Canada where the daughter has qualified for service in the mission field. So the work goes on affecting not only our Highlands and Islands but our cities, our commonwealth and even the mission field."

Kenneth supported that year the establishment of the 87th Glasgow Girls' Brigade and, in addition, was pleased to see the start of Young People's house-groups which met every fortnight for Bible Study and informal discussion. He also encouraged a Sunday afternoon outreach to Foresthall, an old folks' hospital at Cowlairs, where each week various members of the church took it in turn to be involved.

Underlying everything - as his Minister's Message for that year affirmed once more - was prayer. He wrote:

"the Saturday prayer meetings are going to prove a veritable generating station for the supply of power to all our work. Prayer is the price we pay for power. A praying Church is a powerful Church, a progressive Church."

At over eighty years of age, his trust in the Word of God was steadfast, his Christian hope expectant, and his spiritual vision undimmed.

Chapter 8

Last Days

In peace let me resign my breath, and thy salvation see,
My sins deserve eternal death, but Jesus died for me![1]

Apart from an increasing deafness towards the end of his life, Kenneth continued to enjoy a robust lifestyle and a remarkable level of fitness and health. In November 1968, he spent a communion weekend in Kinlochbervie and Durness with the Rev. Jack MacArthur, sharing a room with the Rev. Dr Roddy MacLeod, the current editor of the Gaelic Supplement of the *Life and Work.* Despite the unheated bedroom being so cold that Roddy had to keep his socks on in bed in a vain effort to generate warmth, his room-mate would insist on keeping the window open to let the air in!

In spite of his advancing years, Kenneth's love of ministering in places old and new still flourished. In October 1973, at the age of eighty-six, he therefore made the journey to London to preach at the Church of Scotland's quarterly Gaelic service in Covent Garden.

Back in Glasgow, Kenneth's active support for the evangelical ministries of the city remained strong. The Rev. Douglas MacMillan, on his first evening in the St. Vincent Street Free Church manse following his arrival from Aberdeen, answered the door to find none other than the Gardner Street minister. Moving through to the empty living room, they knelt down on the bare floor where Kenneth proceeded to pray that the Lord would use this new ministry in a mighty way.

On May 24, 1974, a Service of Thanksgiving was held in Gardner Street to mark the fiftieth anniversary of Kenneth's ordination and induction. In a crowded church, chaired by the Session Clerk, Kenneth MacDonald, there were contributions from the Rev. David Barr, who had been minister in Partick St. Mary's (1942-62); the Rev. Angus MacKinnon, almost twenty years in St. Columba's, and the Rev. John Moore, who had by this time moved to Carrubber's Close Mission in Edinburgh. Recognising the strength of Kenneth's association with the police force, Chief Superintendent Tom Carruthers also spoke, standing in for David McNee, the Chief Constable of Glasgow City Police. The Welsh soloist, Clifford Hughes, sang four items of praise, whilst Alasdair N. Macdonald, secretary to the Royal Beatson Hospital, wrote a hymn for the occasion.

Congratulations were received from the churches in Applecross, Carloway, and Tiree, together with messages from the Presbyteries of Lewis and Uist. Personal tributes, too, were read out from the Very Rev. T.M. Murchison and the Very Rev. Andrew Herron.[2] The Free Church Presbytery of Glasgow, and the Moderator of the Free Church, Alastair Ross, Oban, also sent warmest greetings.

A specially commissioned portrait by Kathryn Kynoch, for whom Kenneth had somewhat reluctantly endured several sittings, was then unveiled and presented to him by the longest-serving elder in Gardner Street, Murdo Nicolson. Later, Kenneth was to confide to his immediate family that he'd rather have had a hoover! The portrait never was displayed and, unfortunately, with the passage of time suffered water damage in storage. Following the presentation, Kenneth MacDonald then invited the "real, live, original, and essentially unrepeatable Kenneth Gillies" to address the gathering.[3]

That same weekend the guest preachers in Gardner Street were the Rev. Aonghas I. MacDonald, Barvas, the Rev. John Ferguson, Ness, the Rev. Arthur Wallace, formerly of Blochairn, and the Rev. Donald Macrae, Tarbert. It was a special time for everybody involved.

Almost eighteen months later, Kenneth made arrangements to fly to Lewis to assist at the communion season in Ness. It would be the last time he would visit the island that held such a special place in his heart.

A letter he wrote close to the time bears witness to his ongoing spiritual strength, laced, of course, with characteristic humour and concern for others.

148 Beechwood Drive
September 26, 1975

Dear John Ferguson

Thanks for your note received the other day with all the duties required. You must surely have some Egyptian blood in you when you are such a task-master! However, it will be a pleasure to do as much with your folk as possible. Let us give ourselves to prayer and the ministry of the Word. The apostles withdrawing themselves from other work to give themselves continually to prayer was followed by the number of the disciples multiplying exceedingly. We must pray persistently and believingly. Prayer is power and makes revival certain!

I hope to travel by plane to Stornoway on Tuesday morning and attend a wedding ceremony in the High Church in the afternoon. I will likely stay in town that night.

Many thanks for your kind invitation. Now, my dear sir, I hope you and your good lady and bairns are enjoying good health. I am quite looking forward to my visit to Ness.

With all brotherly regards
Kenneth Gillies

During his trip to Lewis, they made a point of going to Shawbost, the place of Kenneth's missionary endeavours some sixty years previously. Experiencing island hospitality in several homes that day their visit included a call on one woman who had been a child in his Sunday School class way back then. In addition, they were also warmly welcomed at the house in which Kenneth had lodged all those years ago. It was a memorable day.

In the pulpit, too, blessing was evident as Kenneth preached with liberty in both Gaelic and English. Consequently, when the time came for him to leave and catch the flight back to Glasgow, his parting was tinged with sweet sorrow. He would not be back.

The following year, on Friday, February 20, 1976, he presided at what was to be his final Annual Congregational Meeting in Gardner Street. In his message, Kenneth expressed gratitude to God for healthy attendances, reporting that there were one hundred

*Kenneth addresses the congregation during the Service of Thanksgiving
to mark his fifty years in Partick Gardner Street, May 24, 1974.
Left to Right: K. Gillies (grandson), Rev. J. Moore, Rev. D. Barr, K. MacDonald,
Rev. A. MacKinnon, T. Carruthers, C. Hughes, A.K. Gillies.
Dr. K. Taylor, Church Organist, is seated behind.*

and fifty-five members and two hundred and sixty adherents. In particular, he was most encouraged with the numbers who came to the evening services, and exhorted the congregation "to do all that lies in your power to further the word of God in our midst." Once again, he returned to a foundational theme when he declared that God's blessing would be most apparent when the "Church gives itself to importunate wrestling prayer." He concluded with the words from Psalm 90:17 – "And let the beauty of the Lord our God be upon us; And establish Thou the work of our hands upon us; Yea the work of our hands establish Thou it."

Several changes had taken place over the past few years in Gardner Street. The June communion season had been discontinued due to so many of the congregation being away on holiday at that time. The Saturday evening prayer meeting had developed into two groups: one, to serve the continuing Gaelic contingent, met in the lower hall downstairs; the other, which met the desire of those more at home in English, met in the large hall upstairs. In the latter meeting, it was not only men but women, too, who led in prayer.

The Sunday evening service, too, had for some time seen the use of the Redemption Hymnal to supplement the Church Hymnary. And, concurrent with the Gaelic after-meeting, the Youth Fellowship also met.

At the beginning of June 1976, Kenneth left for Applecross. Appropriately, if

Partick Gardner Street Elders, 1974.
Back: H. Gillies, D. MacLeod, C. Morrison, N. Macleod (Penilee), M. MacQuarrie.
Middle: G. Miller, K. Paterson, D. Livingstone, F. MacRitchie, D.J. Smith, J. MacLeod, K. MacDonald.
Front: N. Macleod (Victoria Park), C. MacDonald, M. Nicolson, Rev. K. Gillies, D. MacAulay, M. MacLennan, D. Maclean.

somewhat poignantly, it was to prove to be his last journey to a Highland communion. For the first time in many years he paid a visit to the cemetery at Clachan where his wife, parents, brothers, and sister were buried. Accompanied by his son, Alexander, and the Rev. Finlay MacDonald, Lochluichart, he commented, "How wonderful it will be when all the saved sleeping here will rise together at the resurrection." The evening before returning south he took the prayer meeting in Camusterrach, preaching on the text from Psalm 51:12 – "Restore unto me the joy of thy salvation."

A month later, on Saturday, July 10, Alexander, whilst on holiday in Applecross, made his usual weekly telephone call to Beechwood Drive. Uncharacteristically, his father complained of having had chest pains on and off for a few days. A couple of hours later, Kenneth phoned the church organist, Dr Ken Taylor, who was a consultant cardiologist, and asked him to call. Arriving at the manse, Dr Taylor found him in a semi-collapsed state and somewhat confused.

Over Sunday, nevertheless, he stabilised and by the following morning had recovered sufficiently to rise from his bed and telephone Alexander. What he said to his son, however, was simply to announce that "the time of my departure is at hand" (2 Tim.4:6). On asking if it would be immediate, Alexander gained the impression that his father thought it would be around a fortnight.

That same day, therefore, Alexander, Margaret, and their daughter, Mairi, left Applecross and drove to Glasgow. Unaware that they were coming, Kenneth broke down on seeing them. A lot of tears were shed that evening.

The next day, Kenneth's family doctor, Dr Helen Kennedy, came to the house. Having not been near a doctor's surgery in decades, it had been a job finding out who was his doctor! In fact, Dr Kennedy thought he had died years before! His medical record was blank with nothing having been recorded since the inauguration of the National Health Service in 1948. After examining him, she set the wheels in motion to have him admitted to hospital. That evening, Alexander conducted family worship and, just as in the war years, strength was drawn from the reading of Psalm 91.

On Wednesday morning, having to return to his medical practice in Brora, Alexander said goodbye to his father. Later that day, Kenneth left the Beechwood manse for the last time and was admitted to the Western Infirmary. Here, the diagnosis of a heart attack coupled with pneumonia was confirmed.

A week later, with the medical report looking positive, Kenneth was sitting up in a chair and quite cheerful. However, by the following Saturday, he was once again confined to bed and very tired. Nevertheless, the Rev. John Murdo Smith, who had taken one of the services in Gardner Street the previous Sunday, recalls that Kenneth told him that he had drawn great comfort from the words of Psalm 41:3 - "the Lord will strengthen him upon the bed of languishing: Thou wilt make all his bed in his sickness."

That same day Kenneth also received a visit from the two young ministers, Roddy Morrison and Aonghas Iain MacDonald. He was excited to hear news of a spiritual awakening in the latter's congregation in Barvas and, even when the nurse asked the two of them to leave the room so she could see to her patient, he made sure they'd come back and tell him more!

The next day, though, saw a gradual deterioration in his condition. He had a few visitors including Donald Livingstone, one of his elders from Gardner Street. Before leaving, Kenneth asked him to pray and swung his feet out of the bed to sit beside him. Subsequently, the last person from the congregation to see him was the retired missionary, John Morrison, who was his Gaelic assistant.

At 7.40 a.m., on Monday, July 26, 1976, Kenneth Gillies passed away. It was just as he had indicated to his son two weeks before. Never one to entertain thoughts of retirement he had died "in harness" as he had wished. In the days that followed there were many who mourned the loss of one of whom many said, "there is a prince and a great man fallen this day in Israel" (2 Sam.3:38).

Two days later a Memorial Service was held in Gardner Street conducted by the Rev. A. I. MacDonald. The Order of Service was as follows.

Psalm 23 (Tune: Crimond)

English Prayer - Rev. Arthur Wallace

Readings - from 1 Corinthians 15; Revelation 21

Hymn 701 - What a Friend we have in Jesus (Tune: Blaenwern)

Tribute - Rev. A.I. MacDonald (see Appendix II)

Gaelic Prayer - Rev. Roderick Morrison, North Uist

Gaelic Psalm 107:30-32 (Tune. Coleshill) - Donald J. Smith (Precentor)

Gaelic Benediction

There was a triumphant ring within the church. Many wept unashamedly for the pastor and friend that they had lost. All the Highland presbyterian churches were represented and other denominations besides. Baptists, Brethren, Roman Catholics, all came to pay their respects to a man who "had a big heart, big enough to embrace all God's children of whatever persuasion. [One who] knew no barriers between him and all who shared like faith with himself, [and who breathed] graciousness and zeal for the cause of Christ."[5]

The sun shone brightly as the coffin, held aloft by six of the elders, emerged from the church. Breaking with tradition, they walked with it right down the length of Gardner Street to the corner of Dumbarton Road where the hearse was stationed. People on the streets, in nearby shops and businesses, ail stopped to witness Kenneth Gillies' final goodbye from his beloved Partick.

The next day in Applecross the funeral service in Camusterrach Church of Scotland was led by the Rev. Alasdair MacDonald, Contin, a former minister of the parish. The Order of Service there was as follows.

Gaelic Psalm 73:23-25 (Tune: Torwood) - Donnie Ferguson (Precentor)

Gaelic Prayer - Rev. Duncan Mackinnon, Kyle of Lochalsh

Psalm 23 (Tune: Amazing Grace)

Readings from John 14; Revelation 7, 21 and 22

Tribute - Rev A. MacDonald

English Prayer - Rev. John Moore, Inverness Baptist Church

Psalm 72:17-19 (Tune: Effingham)

Benediction

Following the service, the mourners made their way the few miles north to the cemetery at Clachan on the shores of Applecross Bay. Chief pallbearers were Kenneth's two sons, Alexander and Hector, his grandson, Kenneth, his sister's husband, Danie Beaton, and his first cousin, Alister Gillies. Three other relations, Donnie Ferguson (Milton), Murdo Gillies (Kyle), and Duncan Macbeath (Culduie) made up the complement. At the graveside, the committal was done by the Rev. Finlay MacDonald, Lochluichart, who had shared his final communion in Applecross a few weeks before. Here, at this lovely spot, he was laid to rest.

On August 14, 1976, three tributes to the Rev. Kenneth Gillies appeared in the Stornoway Gazette. One of these was penned by Raymond McKeown, his former assistant, whose description eloquently and with characteristic passion communicates well the essence of the man.

"Mr Gillies was erect in stature, straight in principle, manly in ministry, kindly to the sick and the elderly, compassionate to those in trouble, a great encourager of the young, faithful to his Lord and always abounding in grace.

"He was for generations an institution in Partick - respected by his colleagues, loved by his loyal congregation. He is now a legend - his name writ large in the hearts of all (and they are countless) who were led to the Saviour by him and many are the ministers who are grateful for his encouragement during their fledgling years when with faith and hope and not a little courage he let them loose on the Gardner Street congregation.

"Mr Gillies was a big man, large in his compassion, wide in his sympathies and firm in his judgements. He held stoutly to his own convictions with a becoming humility and with a gracious reticence he refrained from declaiming the different convictions and witness of others. He did this with humour and cheerfulness, with a great fidelity to the faith because he had an anchor for the soul, sure and steadfast within the veil....

"He was a faithful churchman, a good Presbyter, a zealous minister, a sympathetic and diligent pastor, and, above all, a man greatly beloved. He adorned his office. He died as he lived - in Christ."

The Rev. T.M. Murchison, in his memorial tribute in the same newspaper, also spoke for many when he concluded, "only the Great Day will reveal the extent and quality of his influence, directly and indirectly, on unnumbered people."

On the Sunday evening of February 26, 1978, a Memorial Plaque to Kenneth was unveiled in Gardner Street by his son, Hector. It reads:

In cherished memory of the Reverend Kenneth Gillies M.A. who, as preacher, pastor and man of prayer, faithfully served his Lord in this congregation for 52 years, from 29ᵗʰ May 1924, until he was called to glory on 26ᵗʰ July 1976.

"Air chuimhne gu bràth bithidh am fìrean." Salm 112v6

"The righteous shall be in everlasting remembrance."

SERMONS

"By faith . . . he being dead yet speaketh" (Hebs. 11:4)

Three Gaelic Sermons (with translation)

In November 1951 the first live radio broadcast of a Gaelic service took place in Gardner Street. Very positive towards this innovation, Kenneth was to record several sermons over the next twenty-five years.

These first three sermons were broadcast on BBC Radio on successive Sunday afternoons in January 1976 and subsequently printed in *Na Duilleagan Gaidhlig*, the Gaelic supplement to the magazine of the Church of Scotland, *Life and Work*. The editor, the Rev. Thomas Murchison, in an accompanying tribute, commented that in his view they expressed the central substance of the Rev. Kenneth Gillies' preaching.

Sermon 1 - CIOD I BHUR BEATHA?

> *Ciod i bhur beatha? Is deatach i a chithear ré ùine bhig,*
> *agus an déidh sin a théid as an t-sealladh. Seumas 4:14*

Tha bliadhna eile de ar n-ùine air dol seachad, agus tha sinn aig an ám seo 'nar seasamh aig stairsich na bliadhn' ùir, agus tha an t-ám seo iomchuidh gu bhith toirt fa-near cho luath is a tha an ùine a' ruith seachad. *Feuch, rinn tha mar leud bois mo làith'*, mar neoni agad m'aois. Agus tha sinn a' caitheamh ar bliadhnachan mar sgeul a dh'innseadh. "Ciod i bhur beatha?" Tha tri seaghan anns am faod sinn a' cheist a chur.

I

An toiseach, an uair a tha an t-Abstol a' cur na ceiste seo, "Ciod I bhur beatha?", tha e soilleir gu bheil e a' smaoineachadh air a' bheatha aimsireil a tha sinn a' caitheamh anns an t-saoghal seo, oir, an uair a tha e a' freagairt a cheist fhéin, 's e tha e ag ràdh 'na chainnt fhéin, "Is deatach i." Is e sin ri ràdh, anns a' bheatha thalmhaidh aimsireil seo a tha sibh a' cur seachad chan 'eil annaibh ach deatach, ceò, neul, faileas, ag éirigh bho neonaidheachd agus a' teicheadh gu neonaidheachd a rithist. Tha móran shamhlaidhean againn anns an Fhirinn air beatha an duine. Tha Iob ag ràdh, "Bha mo làithean na bu luaithe na gille-ruith; theich iad air falbh; ghabh iad seachad mar na longan luatha, mar an iolaire a' dol air iteig a chum a cobhartaich" - tri samhlaidhean a tha e a' toirt; bho thir, gille-ruith; bho'n mhuir, longan luatha; agus bho'n adhar, iolaire.

Tha beatha an duine a' dol seachad cho luath. Tha e furasda gu leòir dhuinn fhaicinn cho fior is a tha seo, ma smaoinicheas sinn air. Tilg t'inntinn air ais fad na bliadhna a chaidh seachad, agus beachdaich cia meud de do luchd-eòlais a chaidh do'n t-siorruidheachd anns an ùine ghoirid sin. Mar dheatach, mar neul maidne, dh'fhalbh iad as ar sealladh, agus chan fhaic sinn tuilleadh ann an seo iad.

> *Oir gabhaidh thairis osag ghaoith, 's cha bhi e idir ann;*
> *'S chan fhaichear e 'san ionad ud, an robh e fàs gub gu teann.*

Seadh, chan fhada gus an can càch sin m'ar timcheall fhéin. Théid sinne as an t-sealladh mar a chaidh iadsan, oir có an duine a tha beò agus nach fhaic e am bàs, ach is beannaichte na mairbh a gheibh bàs anns an Tighearna a seo a mach.

Nach lìonmhor iad aig a bheil làn-fhios gum feum iad bàsachadh agus a dhol fadheòidh an coinneamh breitheanais, agus, gidheadh, nach d'rinn ullachadh ceart cùramach riamh fa chomhair sin? Thig Là an Tighearna mar ghadaiche 'san oidhche. Cha chuir an gadaiche fios gu bheil e a' tighinn. Chan 'eil fhios againn dé bheir là no uair mun cuairt. Faodaidh the fhéin a bhith air do thoirt air falbh gu h-obann. Bi glic, glac an cothrom. Na bi air do mhealladh, a' gealltainn chothroman dhuit fhéin nach urrainn thu a thoirt dhuit fhéin. Is leòir leis an nàmhaid thu a bhith a' call a' chothroim a tha làthair. Nach 'eil móran ùine luachmhoir air a chall cheana? Cha bheirear air na làithean a dh'fhalbh gu bràth. Cha till iad tuilleadh.

Nach còir dhuinn, ma tà, am beagan làithean a ta romhainn a ghlacadh agus a chur gu buil mhaith? Feuch a nis an t-ám taitneach; feuch a nis là na slàinte. Dean do ghairm agus do thagadh cinnteach. Teagaisg dhuinn ar làithean àireamh a chum gun socraich sinn ar cridhe air gliocas ceart gach tràth.

II

Ach faodaidh sinn a' cheist seo, "Ciod i bhur beatha?", a chur ruinn fhéin ann an seagh na's doimhne. Ciod i bhur beatha? 'S e sin, ciod i an seòrsa beatha a tha thu a' caitheamh o là gu là? An e beatha fheumail urramach a tha a' cuideachadh le maitheas an t-saoghail, air neo an e a chaochladh seòrsa beatha?

Eadhon ann an sealladh nàdurra, gun bruidhinn air diadhaidheachd idir, is e ceist chudthromach a tha seo. Tha e furasda gu leòir do dhaoine a bhith dealbh lethsgeulan dhaibh fhéin air son gnè beatha nach 'eil aona chuid uasal no feumail, a' riarachadh am miannan fhéin agus a' cuartachadh an criochan fhéin. Ach chan 'eil duine sam bith a bheir ceartas do chogais aig nach 'eil fhios nach e sin an seòrsa beatha as uaisle as urrainn duine a chaitheamh. Eadhon anns a' bheatha nàdurra aimsireil tha féin-àicheadh móran na's maisiche agus na's luachmhoire na féin-iarraidh. Tha na h-uile ag iarraidh nan nithean a bhuineas dhaibh fhein, chan iad na nithean a bhuineas do Iosa Criosd.

Ma tha ar beatha anns an t-saoghal seo goirid, nach còir dhuinn seirbhis a dheanamh do'n Tighearna am feadh 's a tha an cothrom againn? Tha obair aig an Tighearna ri dheanamh anns an t-saoghal agus anns an Eaglais, agus tha e ag agairt seirbhis uainn. Air an aobbar sin, gè be ni a gheibh do làmh ri dheanamh, dean e le t'uile dhìcheall, oir chan 'eil obair no innleachd no eòlas no gliocas anns an uaigh d'am bheil thu a' dol. Bi dicheallach an diugh, oir chan fhada gus an bi thu far nach urraunn thu déircean a thoirt uait no dìlleachdain agus bantraichean fhiosrachadh 'nan trioblaid. Cha bhi cothroman agad air son labhairt ri daoine mu thimcheall an anam no an cosnadh gu Criosd. Bitheamaid, ma tà, gnìomhach dileas dùrachdach ann an seirbhis a' Mhaighistir, a' cur gu buil na tàlannan sin a bhuilich e oirnn, eadhon anns na nithean as lugha, a chum gum measar airidh sinn fa-dheòidh air an fhàilte seo, "Is maith, a dheagh sheirbhisich fhìrinnich, imich a steach do aoibhneas do Thighearna."

Cha ghabhar aithreachas gu bràth air son saothair no cruaidh-oibre tre'n téidear air son Aobhar an Tighearna. Chan abair neach aig uair a bhàis, "B'fheàrr nach d'rinn mi saothair cho mór! B'fheàrr nach robh mi ag ùrnuigh cho tric!" Chan abair, ach seallaidh a' mhuinntir seo air an ais le aoibhneas air gach saothair is trioblaid, a' moladh àrdchumhachd Dhé a rinn iadsan a shaoradh o gach trioblaid agus teinn. Is maith a dh'fhaodas sinn uile a ràdh le Pòl, "Tha mi a' meas nach airidh fulangais agus saothair na h-aimsir a ta làthair a bhith air an coimeas ris a' ghlòir a dh'fhoillsichear annainn." Chan 'eil Dia mi-chothromach gun dìochuimnicheadh e obair agus saothair ur gràidh a nochd sibh a thaobh ainme-san. Uime sin, mo bhràithean gràdhach, bithibh-se daingeann neoghluasadach, a' sìor-mheudachadh ann an obair an Tighearna, air dhuibh fios a bhith agaibh nach 'eil ur saothair dìomhain anns an Tighearna.

III

Ach faodaidh sinn ceist an Abstoil, "Ciod i bhur beatha?", a chur ruinn fein ann an seagh na's doimhne fhathast - ann an seagh, nach canadh an t-Abstol idir gur e deatach ur beatha a chithear ré ùine bhig agus an déidh sin théid as an t-sealladh. 'S e theireadh e nach 'eil 'nar beatha ach bith fhìor uasal phearsanta a chaidh a chruthachadh le Dia air son chrìochan àrda, agus is ann anns an t-sealladh seo a tha mórachd is luach na beatha a' tighinn am follais. Chan 'eil aig a' bheatha seo ach aon tobar: *Tobar na beatha tha gu dearbh agadsa, Dhia nan dùl.*

As aonais eòlais air Criosd anns an anam cha bhi aithne no féin-fhiosrachadh againn air a' bheatha seo, ach bheir creideamh ann an Criosd seilbh dhuinn oirre. Tha tobar na beatha againn an uair a tha Criosd annainn. Tha an t-Abstol Eòin ag innse dhuinn sin gu soilleir an uair a tha e ag ràdh, "An tì aig a bheil am Mac tha beatha aige, agus dh'ionnsaich e an leasan sin o'n Mhaighistir fhéin a thubhairt, "Is mise an t-slighe, an fhìrinn, agus a' bheatha."

Bha an t-Abstol Pòl mar an ceudna cinnteach mu'n chùis an uair a sheall e seachad air a' bheatha aimsireil seo a dh'ionnsaigh na sìorruidheachd, ag ràdh, "An uair a dh'fhoillsichear Criosd, neach as e ar beatha-ne, ann an sin foillsichear sinne maille ris ann an glòir.

Iarramaid, ma tà, seilbh ann an Criosd a chum 's gum bi sinn comasach air a ràdh, "'S e Criosd mo bheatha-sa, oir tha Criosd beò annam, agus tha mise beò annsan agus bithidh gu sìorruidh. Cha deatach mo bheatha-sa idir a chithear air son ùine bhig agus an déidh sin a théid as an t-sealladh, ach beatha mhaireannach ann an comunn ris an Athair, a' Mhac, agus an Spiorad Naomh. Ma's urrainn sinn a leithid sin de dh'aidmheil a dheanamh a nis, cha diochuimhnich sinn a' bheatha a tha mar dheatach, ach oidhirpichidh sinn air feum as fheàrr a dheanamh dhith cho fhad 's a tha i againn. Gum beannaicheadh an Tighearna dhuinn a bhith smaoineachadh air Fhocal naomh fhéin.

(Gaelic Sermon 1 - WHAT IS YOUR LIFE?)

> *For what is your life? It is even a vapour, that appeareth for a little time,*
> *and then vanisheth away. James 4:14.*

Another year of our life has gone, and we are now standing on the threshold of a New Year, an appropriate moment to appreciate how quickly time is passing by. "Behold, Thou hast made my days as an handbreadth; and mine age is as nothing before Thee" (Ps.39:5). "We spend our years as a tale that is told" (Ps.90:9). What is your life? There are three ways in which we can pose this question.

I

Firstly, when the Apostle puts this question "What is your life?" it is clear that he is thinking about the temporal life that we spend in this world, for when he answers his own question he says that, "It is a vapour." That is to say, in this passing earthly life we are but a vapour, mist, a cloud, a shadow, rising from nothing and dispersing into nothingness again. God's Word provides us with many analogies for human life. Job 9:25-26 says, "Now my days are swifter than a post: they flee away, they see no good. They are passed away as the swift ships: as the eagle that hasteth to the prey." Three comparisons; from the land, a post or messenger; from the sea, swift ships; and from the sky, an eagle.

Human life passes very quickly. It is easy enough for us to appreciate how true this is, if we but think about it. Cast your mind back over the year that has gone, and consider how many of your acquaintances have gone into eternity during that short time. Like mist, like a morning cloud, they have gone from our sight, and we shall not see them here again:

> *For over it the wind doth pass, and it away is gone;*
> *And of the place where once it was, it shall no more be known.*

And truly it will not be long till others say that about us. We shall disappear as they have done, for what man living shall not see death, but "blessed are the dead who die in the Lord" (Rev.14:13).

Are there not many who know full well that they must die and in the end face judgement, but who, nevertheless, have made no true and careful preparation for that day? "The Day of the Lord will come as a thief in the night" (2 Pet.3:10). The thief does not give advance notice of his coming. We do not know what a day or an hour will bring forth. You yourself may be suddenly called away. Be wise and seize the opportunity. Don't be deceived, promising yourself opportunities that you cannot give yourself. The Enemy is content if you only lose the present opportunity. Hasn't much valuable time been lost already? The days that are gone can never be recovered, they will not return.

Ought we not, then, to seize the few days that are left to us and put them to good use? "Behold, now is the accepted time: behold, now is the day of salvation" (2 Cor.6:2). "Make your calling and election sure" (2 Pet.1:10). "Teach us to number our days, that we may apply our hearts unto wisdom" (Ps.90:12).

II

But we may apply this question "What is your life?" to ourselves in a deeper sense. What *is* your life? What sort of life are you living from day to day? Is it a useful, honourable life that contributes to the good of the world, or is it an entirely different kind of life? Even on a natural level, without considering godliness at all, this is an important question. It is easy enough for people to fabricate excuses for themselves for the kind of life that is neither noble nor useful, satisfying their own desires and seeking their own ends. But there is no one who gives due place to his conscience who does not know that that is not the noblest kind of life a man can live. Even in our natural earthly life, self-denial is much more attractive and valuable than self-seeking. *For all seek their own, not the things which are Jesus Christ's.*

If our life in this world is short, ought we not to serve the Lord while we have the opportunity? The Lord has work to do in the world and in the Church, and he requires service from us. Therefore, "whatsoever thy hand findeth to do, do it with thy might; for there is no work, nor device, nor knowledge, nor wisdom, in the grave, whither thou goest" (Ecc.9:10). Be diligent today, for you will soon be where you can neither give alms nor visit orphans and widows in their affliction. You will have no opportunities to speak to people about their soul's need, or to win them for Christ. Let us, then, be diligent, faithful and earnest in the Master's service, using those talents that he has given us, even in the smallest things, so that in the end we may be judged worthy of this welcome: "Well done, thou good and faithful servant: enter thou into the joy of thy Lord" (Matt.25:21).

Any labour or hardship endured for the Lord's cause will never be regretted. No one will say at the hour of his death, "I wish I hadn't laboured so hard! I wish I hadn't prayed so often!" No, but these people will look back with joy on every toil and suffering, praising the mighty power of God that delivered them from every trouble and affliction. Well might we all say along with Paul: "I reckon that the sufferings of this present time are not worthy to be compared with the glory which shall be revealed in us" (Rom.8:18). God is not unjust, that he should forget the work and labour of your love which you have shown in his name. "Therefore, my beloved brethren, be ye steadfast, unmoveable, always abounding in the work of the Lord, forasmuch as ye know that your labour is not in vain in the Lord" (1 Cor.15:58).

III

But we may apply the Apostle's question "What is your life?" to ourselves in a still deeper sense. In this sense, the Apostle would not say that our life is a vapour that appears for a short time and then vanishes away. Rather, he would say that our life is a truly noble, personal existence created by God for higher ends, and it is in this light that the greatness and worth of life is seen. This life has only one fountain: *Because of life, the fountain pure remains alone with thee.*

Without knowledge of Christ in the soul, we can have no knowledge or experience of this life. We have the fountain of life when we have Christ within us. The Apostle John clearly tells us that when he says, "He who hath the Son hath life" (1 John 5:12); and he learned that lesson from the Master Himself who said, "I am the way, the truth, and the life" (John 14:6). The Apostle Paul, too, was sure of this when he said "when Christ, who is our life, shall appear, then shall ye also appear with him in glory" (Col.3:4).

Let us therefore seek to have a possession in Christ so that we may be able to say, "Christ is my life, for Christ lives in me, and I am alive in him and shall be for ever. My life is no vapour that appears for a short time and then vanishes away, but an eternal life in fellowship with the Father, the Son and the Holy Spirit." If we can make such a confession as that now, then we shall not disregard the life that is like a vapour, but we shall endeavour to make the best use of it as long as we have it.

May God bless to us our meditation on his own sacred word.

Sermon 2 - THIGEAMAID GU RIGH-CHATHAIR NAN GRAS

Thigeamaid uime sin le dànachd gu rìgh-chathair nan gràs,
a chum gum faigh sinn tròcair,
agus gun amais sinn air gras a chum cobhair ann an am feuma. Eabhr 4:16

Is e ùrnuigh a bhith cur suas ar n-achaingean ri Dia, ag iarraidh nithean a réir a thoile ann an ainm Chriosd, ag aideachadh ar peacannan, agus a' toirt buidheachais dha air son a thròcairean. Thug Criosd aitè ro-àrd agus ro-urramach do dhleasdanas 'na h-ùrnuigh 'na chaithe-beatha agus 'na theagasg. Tharladh, an uair a bha Iosa air a bhaisteadh, agus e ri ùrnuigh, gun do dh'fhosgladh nèamh. Air Beinn a' Chruth-atharrachaidh, an uair a bha e ri ùrnuigh, bha dreach a ghnùis air atharrachadh agus rinneadh eudach geal agus dealrach. Aig ám eile chaidh e suas gu beinn a dheanamh ùrnuigh, agus bhuanaich e ré na h-oidhche ann an ùrnuigh ri Dia.

Chan 'eil ach dà nì a tha gu neo-sheachanta feumail ann an ùrnuigh, agus tha an dà nì seo air an toirt f'ar comhair anns na briathran seo leis an Abstol. "Is éiginn do'n tì a thig a dh'ionnsaigh Dhé a chreidsinn gu bheil e ann, agus gur e an tì e a bheir duais do'n dream a dh'iarras e gu dìcheallach." Ma tha thu a' creidsinn gu bheil Dia ann, ma tha thu a' creidsinn gur e an tì e a dh'éisdeas urnuigh, ma tha thu a' dòrtadh a mach do chridhe 'na làthair agus ag earbsa 'na ghealladh, ann an sin tha t'ùrnuigh fìor agus ceart, agus gu cinnteach freagraidh Dia i. "Thigeamaid uime sin le dànachd gu rìgh-chathair nan gràs, a chum gum faigh sinn tròcair, agus gun amais sinn air gràs a chum cobhair ann an ám feuma."

I

Beachdaich, an toiseach, air a' chleachdadh spioradail a dh'ionnsaigh a bheil sinn air ar gairm. "Thigeamaid gu rìgh-chathair nan gràs."

'S e a' chathair seo cathair Dhé, air a bbeil an t-Athair 'na shuidhe, agus am Mac aig a dheas-làimh - cathair móralachd agus glòir Dhé bhios là-eigin 'na cathair breitheanais. Theirear cathair gràis ris a' chathair seo an diugh a chionn agus gur e seo linn nan gràs. Tha Dia nan gràs 'na shuidhe air a' chathair seo. Tha e feitheamh ri bhith gràsmhor, agus tha an t-slighe fosgailte do neach sam bith a tha a' cur feum air tròcair a thighinn a steach a dh'ionnsaigh làthaireachd Dhé. Dean faire chum ùrnuigh. Dean ùrnuigh gun sgur. Cha leig thu a leas dàil a chur ann an ùrnuigh a dheanamh gus an téid do'n eaglais; faodaidh tu ùrnuigh a dheanamh anns na h-uile àite. Tha an Tighearna a ghnàth ag éisdeachd ri úrnuighean pheacach bochda. Tha a chluas an còmhnaidh fosgailte. An uair a nì thu ùrnuigh, imich a steach do do sheòmar, agus air dùnadh do dhoruis duit dean ùrnuigh ri t'Athair a tha ann an uaigneas, agus bheir t'Athair a chì ann an uaigneas duais dhuit gu follaiseach. Mar a tha sinn a' dlùthachadh ri cathair gràis, an uair a tha sinn a' togail suas ar n-anama ri Dia ann an spiorad agus ann am fìrinn ann an ùrnuigh. Agus 's e sin an cleachdadh gus a bheil ar ceann-teagaisg 'gar gairm. "Thigeamaid am fagus gu rìghchathair nan gràs."

A bheil an cleachdadh seo agad féin? An uair a dh'éireas tu anns a'mhadainn, a bheil e 'na chleachdadh agad do ghlùn a lùbadh an làthair Dhé? Nach truagh an duine no a'bhean a tha gun ùrnuigh! Feumar ùrnuigh a chleachdadh mar mheadhon air a bhith beò tre chreideamh ann an Criosd a réir an duine nuaidh. Tha Dia ag iarraidh seo. Deanaibh ùrnuigh gun sgur. Is e Dia fear-éisdeachd ùrnuigh. "O thusa a dh'éisdeas ri ùrnuigh, thugadsa thig gach feòil." Tha daoine nach dean ùrnuigh marbh do Dhia. Tha ùrnuigh air a cur air thoiseach air gach seirbhis eile a nì duine do Dhia. Tha na geallaidhean a tha air an toirt do chreideamh air an toirt do ùrnuigh mar an ceudna, oir tha an Sgriobtur ag ràdh, "Ge bè neach a chreideas annsan, cha nàraichear e, agus ge bè neach a ghairmeas air ainm an Tighearna, teàrnar e." Tre'n ùrnuigh tha sinn a' cleachdadh gràis agus a' faotainn gràis agus naomhachd.

II

Beachdaich anns an dara àite, air an spiorad anns an còir dhuinn tighinn dlùth. "Thigeamaid le dànachd."

Tha e 'na nì iongantach gum biodh cead aig creutairean cho peacach ruinne ùrnuigh a dheanamh. An uair a bheir sinn fa-near ciod a tha sinn agus có e Dia, dh'fhaodadh eagal a bhith oirnn, trath thig sinn d'a ionnsaigh, gun cuireadh e cùl ruinn, mur biodh e 'gar misneachadh gu tighinn eadhon le dànachd. Chan 'eil seo a' ciallachadh gu bheil sinn ri teachd gun urram agus gun irioslachd, ach gu bheil sinn ri ùrmuigh a dheanamh le lànchinnteachd gun éisd Dia ruinn.

"A mhuinntir mo ghràidh, mur dìt ar cridhe sinn, tha dànachd againn a thaobh Dhé, agus ge bè nì a dh'iarras sinn gheibh sinn uaithe e, do bhrìgh gu bheil sinn a' coimhead àithntean agus a' deanamh nan nithean a tha taitneach 'na fhianais. Feumaidh an dànachd gu bheil sinn air ar gairm a bhith air a bonndachadh gu buileach air tròcair Dhé ann an Criosd, agus tha sin a' giùlan leis dá smuain.

An toiseach, beò-mhothachadh air neo-airidheachd. Tha mothachadh peacaidh 'na eileamaid do-sheachnaichte ann an dànachd shoisgeulach. Tha sinn a' call urram do Dhia, an uair a tha sinn a' call lorg air ar peacaidhean. 'S e mothachadh peacaidh, ma tà, a' cheud eileamaid anns an dànachd gus a bheil sinn air ar gairm, ach 's e an dara eileamaid agus an eileamaid chudthromach mothachadh soilleir spioradail air luach ìobairt Chriosd. 'S e seo fìor ghrunnd ar dànachd.

An uair a tha am peacach a' tuigsinn gun d'rinn Dia ann an Criosd réite air son ar peacaidhean, agus gu bheil Fear-saoraidh beò aig deas-làimh Dhé air a' chathair, gu bheil Dia air sgàth Chriosd a' maitheadh pheacaidhean, agus 'gan cur gu bràth as a shealladh, tha dànachd aig an duine sin ann a bhith tighinn dlùth. Seo far a bheil creideamh a' faotainn cleachdadh. An creideamh nach 'eil a' toirt leis ach mothachadh peacaidh, chan fhaigh sinn uaithe ach eòlas air dìteadh. An creideamh a tha a' teàrnadh agus a bheir comhfhurtachd, sin an creideamh a tha a' faicinn luach ìobairt Chriosd agus a' socrachadh air; agus, ged a tha beò-mhothachadh aige air na tha am peacadh a' toilltinn, tha e a' faicinn gu bheil tròcair Dhé na's motha na am peacadh.

III

Beachdaich a nis, anns an treas àite, air na beannachdan a shealbhaicheas sinn tre bhith a' tarraing dlùth - "a chum gum faigh sinn tròcair, agus gun amais sinn air gràs a chum cobhair ann an ám feuma" - dà bheannachd mhór, tròcair agus gràs.

Faodaidh e bhith fìor gu bheil amannan nar beatha anns a bheil sinn na's feumaiche na aig amannan eile, agus tha gealladh againn a thaobh nan amannan sin, gum fritheil Dia gràs ruinn a réir ar feum. Nì e maille ris a' bhuaireadh slighe gu dol as tre'm faigh sinn saorsa. Ach 's e an t-ám feuma 'nar ceann-teasgaig an t-ám a tha làthair. Tha Dia air cathair gràis a nis. Tha feum againn air gràs a nis. Tha dorus nèimh fosgailte an diugh. Thig a nis! 'S e a' mhionaid a tha làthair ám ar cothroim, fhad 's a tha Dia 'na shuidhe air cathair gràis agus chan ann air cathair breitheanais. Iarraibh an Tighearna am feadh a tha e ri fhaotainn.

Faodaidh e bhith gu bheil tròcair ag amharc ri ar feum air maitheanas mar pheacaich chiontach. Ma dh'aidicheas sinn ar peacaidhean, tha esan firinneach agus ceart a chum ar peacaidhean a mhaitheadh dhuinn agus ar glanadh o gach uile neo-fhìreantachd.

Faodaidh e bhith gu bheil gràs a' sealltainn ri ar feum air cuideachadh 'nar beatha Chrìosdail. Tha sinn anns an dà sheagh seo an còmhnaidh a' seasamh ann an feum air cobhair o Dhia. Tha e feumail gum fàs sinn ann an gràs. 'S e toradh an Spioraid gràdh, aoibhneas, sìth, fad-fhulangas, caomhalachd, maitheas, creideamh, macantas, agus stuaim. Ach nach fheum sinn a bhith ag aideachadh gu bheil iomadh nì anns a' chridhe a tha a' cathachadh an aghaidh nan gràsan seo? Faodaidh an neach as inbhiche ann an gràs a bhith ag ràdh maille ri Pòl, "Tha ni a' faicinn lagh eile 'nam bhuill a' cogadh an aghaidh lagh m'inntinn, agus 'gam thoirt am bruid do lagh a' pheacaidh a tha 'nam bhuill. Och, is duine truagh mi! Cò á shaoras mi o chorp a' bhàis seo?

Ach chan fhaod sinn a bhith air ar leagadh sios le dìobhail-misnich. Deanamaid faire an aghaidh peacaidh agus an aghaidh buairidh. Deanamaid ùrnuigh. Cuireamaid ar n-earbsa ann an Criosd, agus bheir e dhuinn buaidh agus tuilleadh agus buaidh thar gach nàmhaid. Tha Dia gràsmhor. 'S e fear-éisdeachd ùrnuigh. Tha eadar-mheadhonair againn a choisinn slàinte air ar son, a phàidh ar fiachan uile, agus a tha a ghnàth a' deanamh eadar-ghuidhe air ar son. Nach fhaod sinn, ma tà, a bhith a' tighinn gu rìgh-chathair nan gràs le dànachd, iriosal, a chum agus gum faigh sinn tròcair, agus gun amais sinn air gràs a chum cobhair ann an àm feuma.

Gum beannaicheadh an Tighearna dhuinn a bhith a' smaoineachadh air fhìrinn.

(Gaelic Sermon 2 - LET US COME TO THE THRONE OF GRACE)

Let us therefore come boldly unto the throne of grace,
that we may obtain mercy,
and find grace to help in time of need. Hebrews 4:16

Prayer is a raising of our requests to God, asking for things according to his will in the name of Christ, confessing our sins, and giving him thanks for his mercies. Christ gave a very high and honourable place to the duty of prayer both in his life and in his teaching. When Jesus was baptised, and praying, Heaven was opened. On the Mount of Transfiguration, when he was praying, the appearance of his face was changed, and his garments became white and dazzling. At another time, he went up a mountain to pray, and continued all night in prayer to God.

There are only two things that are absolutely indispensable in prayer, and both of them are brought before us in these words of the Apostle: "He that cometh to God must believe that he is, and that he is a rewarder of them that diligently seek him" (Heb.11:6). If you believe that God exists, if you believe that he is the hearer of prayer, if you pour out your heart in his presence and rely upon his promise, then your prayer is right and true, and assuredly God will answer it. "Let us therefore come boldly unto the throne of grace, that we may obtain mercy, and find grace to help in time of need."

I

Consider, first, the spiritual practice to which we are called: "Let us come to the throne of grace."

This throne is the throne of God, on which the Father sits with the Son at his right hand - the throne of the majesty and glory of God, which will one day become the throne of Judgment. Today, this throne is called a throne of grace because this is the age of grace. The God of grace sits on this throne. He waits to be gracious, and the way is open for anyone who needs mercy to come into the presence of God. Watch and pray. Pray without ceasing. You do not have to delay praying until you go to church; you may pray in any place. The Lord always hears the prayers of the poor sinners. His ear is ever open. "When you pray, enter into thy closet and, when thou hast shut thy door, pray to the Father which is in secret, and thy Father which seeth in secret shall reward thee openly" (Matt.6:6). As we draw near to the throne of grace, then we lift up our soul to God in spirit and in truth as we pray. And that is the practice to which our text calls us, "Let us come to the throne of grace."

Is this your practice? When you rise in the morning, is it your custom to bend your knee in the presence of God? Pity the man or woman who never prays! Prayer must be used as a means whereby the renewed person can live by faith in Christ. God requires this. Pray without ceasing. God is the hearer of prayer. "0 thou that hearest prayer, unto thee shall all flesh come" (Ps.65:2). People who do not pray are dead towards God.

Prayer takes precedence over every other service that a person renders to God. The promises made to faith are also made to prayer, for Scripture says: "Whosoever believeth on him shall not be ashamed . . and whosoever shall call upon the name of the Lord shall be saved" (Rom.10:11,13). Through prayer we exercise grace and in turn receive grace and holiness.

II

Consider, in the second place, the spirit in which we ought to draw near. "Let us come with boldness."

It is an amazing thing that creatures as sinful as we are should be permitted to pray. When we realise what we are and who God is, we might fear that, when we come to him, he might reject us, were it not that he encourages us to come, even with boldness. This does not mean that we are to come without reverence and humility, but rather that we are to pray with the full assurance that God will hear us.

"Beloved, if our heart condemn us not, then we have confidence toward God. And whatsoever we ask, we receive of him, because we keep his commandments, and do those things that are pleasing in his sight" (1 John 3:21,22). The boldness we are called upon to exercise must be based entirely on the mercy of God in Christ, and that carries with it two thoughts.

First, a lively awareness of our unworthiness. Awareness of sin is an indispensable element in evangelical boldness. We lose reverence for God when we lose sight of our sins. Consciousness of sin, then, is the first element in the boldness we are urged to exercise, and the second, vital ingredient is a clear spiritual apprehension of the worth of Christ's sacrifice. This is the true ground of our boldness.

When the sinner understands that God in Christ has made atonement for our sins, that there is a living Saviour at the right hand of God on the throne, that God for Christ's sake forgives sins and forever banishes them from his sight, then that person has boldness to draw near. This is when faith is exercised. The faith that brings with it nothing but awareness of sin can only receive awareness of condemnation. The faith that saves and brings comfort is the faith that sees the value of Christ's sacrifice and rests on it; and though it has a lively awareness of all that sin deserves, it sees that God's mercy is greater than sin.

III

Consider now, in the third place, the blessings we possess through drawing near: "That we may obtain mercy, and find grace to help in time of need". Two great blessings: mercy and grace.

It may be that there are times in our lives when we are in greater need than at other times, and we have a promise regarding those times that God will give us grace according to our need. He will make with the temptation a way of escape. But the time of need in our text is the present time. God is on the throne of grace now. We need grace now. The door of heaven is open now. Come now! The present moment is the time of our opportunity, while God is sitting on a throne of grace and not on a throne of judgement. Seek the Lord while he may be found.

Maybe mercy has to do with our need of forgiveness as guilty sinners. "If we confess our sins, he is faithful and just to forgive our sins, and to cleanse us from all unrighteousness" (1 John 1:9). Possibly, grace has to do with our need of help in living our Christian lives.

In these two senses we are always in need of God's help. It is necessary that we grow in grace. "The fruit of the Spirit is love, joy, peace, longsuffering, gentleness, goodness, faith, meekness, temperance" (Gal.5:22-23). But don't we have to admit that there are many things in our hearts which war against this grace? Even the person who has reached the highest level in grace can still say, along with Paul: "I see another law in my members, warring against the law of my mind, and bringing me into captivity to the law of sin which is in my members. 0 wretched man that I am! Who shall deliver me from the body of this death?" (Rom.7:23-24).

But we must not be cast down in despair. Let us be vigilant against sin and temptation. Let us pray. Let us put our trust in Christ, and he will make us more than victors over every enemy. God is gracious, he is the hearer of prayer. We have a Mediator who has purchased salvation for us, who has paid all our debts, and who ever intercedes for us. May we not, then, come to the throne of grace with a humble boldness, so that we may obtain mercy, and find grace to help in time of need. May God bless to us our meditation on his truth.

Sermon 3 - DUTHAICH AS FEARR

Ach a nis tha déidh aca air dùthaich as feàrr. Eabhr. 11:16

Ghairm Dia Abraham, ag ràdh ris, "Rach a mach o d' dhùthaich agus o d' dhìlsibh agus á taigh, t'athar do'n tìr a nochdas mise dhuit," agus dh'imich e a mach air àithne an Tighearna. Cha do phill e air ais tuilleadh. Chan e nach fhaodadh e, oir, nam biodh e cuimhneachail air an dùthaich sin as an deach e mach, dh'fhaodadh e ám iomchuidh a ghabhail gu pilleadh. Ach roghnaich e a bhith air chuairt ann am pàilliunaibh maille ri Isaac agus Iacob, co-oighreachan a' gheallaidh cheudna. Bha iad sin uile beò tre chreideamh. Bha déidh aca air dùthaich as feàrr, dùthaich nèamhaidh.

A nis, tha an suidheachadh a tha againne anns an t-saoghal seo cosmhail ris an tsuidheachadh a bha acasan. Tha a' mheud dhinn is a ghabh ri Criosd air ar gairm a mach. "Air an aobhar sin rachamaid a mach d'a ionnsaigh-san an taobh a muigh de'n champ, a' giùlan a mhaslaidh-san." Chan e an saoghal seo ar dachaigh; 's ann tha ar dachaigh shuas. Tha sinn ag amharc air a son am measg nan nithean nach faicear. Tha sinn 'nar coigrich agus luchd-cuairt air an talamh.

Ann a bhith a' beachdadachd air na briathran seo, tha mi a' rùnachadh a bhith a' nochdadh cionnas a tha an dùthaich seo 'na dùthaich as feàrr.

Nach 'eil, anns a' cheud àite, a chionn gu bheil fois shìorruidh r'a mealtainn innte? "Anns an t-saoghal seo bithidh àmhghar agaibh." Ach tha e fìor gu bheil fois anns an tsaoghal cuideachd. Tha an Sgriobtur a' labhairt air iomadh seòrsa fois. "Is truagh dhaibhsan a tha gu suaimhneach ann an Sion." Sin muinntir a tha marbh gu spioradail. Ach an t-anam a thàinig gu Criosd, fhuair e fois. "Thigibh a m'ionnsaigh-sa, sibhse uile a tha ri saothair agus fo throm uallaich agus bheir mi suaimhneas dhuibh. Gabhaibh mo chuing oirbh agus fòghlumaibh uam, oir tha mise macanta agus iriosal ann an cridhe, agus gheibh sibh fois do bhur n-anamaibh." Mur tig e 'gad ionnsaigh-sa anns a' bheatha seo, chan fhaigh thu e troimh an t-sìorruidheachd. Mar thubhairt aon de na naoimh, "Chan 'eil ni ann an Glòir aca nach d'fhuair iad a shìol anns an t-saoghal."

Tha an dùthaich nèamhaidh, mar an ceudna 'na dùthaich as feàrr a chionn na slàinte shìorruidh a tha innte. Tha e air innse dhuinn nach téid tinneas no bròn no bàs a steach innte. Chan abair am fear-àiteachaidh, "Tha mi tinn." Bidh an corp a dh'éireas as an uaigh 'na chorp neo-thruaillidh, agus cha mhothaich e gu bràth pian no sgìos no crìonadh. Agus ni as feàrr na seo uile, cha bhi peacadh tuilleadh ann. Cha toir buaidh a' pheacaidh air seachran iad na's mò.

Tha an dùthaich nèamhaidh 'na dùthaich as feàrr a chionn na cuideachd a bhios innte. Bidh aoibhneas agus gàirdeachad orra ann an comunn a chéile, agus gabhaidh Dia fhéin còmhnaidh 'nam measg. Bidh naoimh nan ceud-linntean an siud - na martaraich, na h-abstoil, agus na fàidhean. An siud mar an ceudna coinnichidh sinn ainglean agus àrdainglean agus - na's feàrr na sin - chì sinn Iosa 'na dhaonnachd ghlòirichte. Chì sinn a ghnùis agus bithidh sinn gu bràth maille ris an Tighearna.

A nis, cionnas a thàinig iad seo gu déidh a bhith aca air an dùthaich nèamhaidh? Nach tàinig le bhith a' cluinntinn m'a timcheall? Cionnas a chreideas iad anns an Tì air nach cual iad iomradh? Is e creideamh brìgh nan nithean ri'm bheil dòchas, dearbhchinnte nan nithean nach faicear. Tha ar cridheachan air an aonadh ri Criosd air a leithid de dhòigh is gu bheil ar caithne-beatha air nèamh. Mar a thuirt bean air leabaidh a bàis, "Tha mo cheann an nèamh, tha mo chridhe an nèamh; ceum eile agus bidh mi gu hiomlan ann an nèamh!"

Cionnas, ma tà, a tha an déidh seo air an dùthaich nèamhaidh 'ga foillseachadh 'nar beatha? Nach 'eil anns a' mheas a tha againn oirre? "Na nithean," arsa Pòl, "a bha 'nam buannachd dhomh, mheas mi iad sin 'nan call air son Chriosd." Agus bhuanaich e de'n inntinn sin a dh'aindeoin na dh'fhuiling e, agus e a nis 'na phrìosanach anns an Ròimh, ceangailte ri saighdear le slabhraidh, agus am bas a' bagradh air a h-uile là. Nach cuimhne leibh mar a thuirt e, "Seadh, gun amharas, agus tha mi a' meas nan uile nithean 'nan call air son ro-òirdhearcas eòlas Iosa Chriosd mo Tighearna, air son an d'fhuiling mi call nan uile nithean, agus tha mi a' meas gur aolach iad a chum gun coisninn Criosd." Sin agaibh fear aig an robh déidh air an dùthaich nèamhaidh.

Tha an déidh seo 'ga taisbeanadh fhéin gu sònraichte anns an t-saothair a tha sinn a' deanamh gu bhith a' mealtainn Rìoghachd Dhé. Tha e fìor nach teàrnar sinn le ar noibre fhéin. Tha e co-ionnan fìor nach bi sinn air ar teàrnadh as eugmhais oibre, oir mar a tha an corp marbh as eugmhais an spioraid, mar an ceudna tha creideamh marbh as eugmhais oibre. Cluinn an nì a tha Pòl ag ràdh faisg air crìch a thuruis: "Chòmhraig mi an deagh chòmhrag; chrìochnaich mi mo thurus; ghléidh mi an creideamh; o seo a mach taisgear fa mo chomhair crùn fireantàchd a bheir an Tighearna, am Britheamh cothromach, dhomh, anns an là ud, agus chan ann dhòmhsa a mháin, ach dhaibh-san uile mar an ceudna leis an ionmhainn a theachd-san."

Is e Dia féin a ta ag innse dhuinn gum feumar spàirn chruaidh a dheanamh leis gach uile neach a chum ruigsinn air an dùthaich as feàrr. "Deanaibh spàirn chruaidh gu dol a steach air a' gheata chumhann, oir tha mi ag radh ruibh gun iarr móran dol a steach agus nach urrainn iad." "Deanaibh tuilleadh dìchill chum bhur gairm agus bhur taghadh a dheanamh cinnteach."

Is ann do'n tì a bhuadhaicheas a bheir Criosd r'a ithe de'n mhana fholaichte, agus bheir e dha clach gheal, agus air a' chloich ainm nuadh sgrìobhte nach aithne do neach air bith ach do'n ti a gheibh i; ithidh e de chraoibh na beatha a tha ann am meadhon Pàrrais Dhé, agus cha chiùrrar leis an dara bàs e. Aidichidh Criosd 'ainm-san ann am fianais 'Athar agus am fianais 'ainglean-san, agus ni e e 'na phost ann an Teampull Dhé, agus cha téid e na's motha a mach as, agus sgrìobhaidh e ainm a Dhé air, agus ainm cathrach a Dhé as i Ierusalem Dhé a thig a nuas o nèamh o a Dhia, agus sgrìobhaidh e 'ainm nuadh féin air - seadh, bheir e comas dha suidhe maille ris air a rìgh-chathair, amhail fòs a bhuadhaich e fhéin agus a shuidhe e maille r'a Athair air a rìgh-chathair-san. An tì aig a bheil cluas, éisdeadh e ciod a tha an Spiorad ag ràdh ris na h-eaglaisean.

> *0, gum biodh mo spiorad ullamh,*
> *Air a ghréiseadh mar le h-òr,*
> *Is air éideadh leis a' chulaidh*
> *'S cubhaidh do'n a' mhuinntir chòir;*
> *Le mo lòchran air a lasadh,*
> *Agus ola 'na stòr,*
> *Gu dhol staigh leis gus an t-suipeir,*
> *Nuair a thig e air mo thòir.*

Có nach deanadh saothair agus nach gabhadh an rathad a tha a' treòrachadh a dh'ionnsaigh na dùthcha as feàrr?

(Gaelic Sermon 3 – A BETTER COUNTRY)

It was a version of this sermon that Kenneth preached in Applecross Church of Scotland on the Sunday which fell between Molly's death and her funeral in January 1946.

> *But now they desire a better country. Hebrews 11:16*

God called Abraham, saying to him, "Get thee out of thy country, and from thy kindred, and from thy father's house, and unto a land that I will shew thee" (Gen.12:1). And he went out at the Lord's command. He did not return again. It was not that he could not, for if he had been mindful of that country from whence he came out, he might have had opportunity to have returned. But he chose to dwell in tents along with Isaac and Jacob, fellow-heirs of the same promise. They were all living by faith. They desired a better country, that is, a heavenly one.

Now, our situation in this world is similar to theirs. Those of us who have received Christ are called to go out: "Let us go forth therefore unto him without the camp, bearing his reproach" (Heb.13:13). This world is not our home; our home is above. We look for it among the things that are invisible. We are strangers and pilgrims on the earth.

In contemplating these words, my purpose is to show how this country is a better country.

Is this not so, in the first place, because eternal rest is to be enjoyed in it? "In the world ye shall have tribulation" (John 16:33). But it is true that there is rest in the world as well. Scripture speaks of many kinds of rest. "Woe to them that are at ease in Zion" (Amos 6:1). These are people who are spiritually dead. But the soul who has come to Christ has truly received rest. "Come unto me, all ye that labour and are heavy laden, and I will give you rest. Take my yoke upon you, and learn of me, for I am meek and lowly in heart, and ye shall find rest unto your souls" (Matt.11:28-29). If you do not find it here in this life, you will not possess it in eternity. As one of the saints remarked, "They have nothing in Glory but the seed of which they received in the world."

The heavenly country is also a better country because of the eternal salvation it contains. We are told that neither sickness nor sorrow nor death shall enter it. The inhabitant shall not say, "I am sick". The body that will rise from the grave will be an imperishable body, and it will never experience pain or weariness or decay. And better than all of this, there will be no more sin. The power of sin will no more lead them astray.

The heavenly country is a better country on account of the company to be found there. They will experience joy and rejoicing in each other's fellowship, and God himself will dwell among them. The saints of the early ages will be there - the martyrs, apostles and prophets. There, too, we shall meet angels and archangels, and - better still - we shall see Jesus in his glorified manhood. We shall see his face and we shall be forever with the Lord.

Now, how did these people come to have a desire for the heavenly country? Surely it was by hearing about it. "How shall they believe in him of whom they have not heard?" (Rom.10:14). "Faith is the substance of things hoped for, the evidence of things not seen" (Heb.11:1). Our hearts are united to Christ in such a way that our citizenship is in Heaven. As a woman said on her deathbed, "My head is in Heaven, my heart is in Heaven; another step and I shall be entirely in Heaven!"

How, then, does this desire for a better country manifest itself in our lives? Is it not in the value we place upon it? "What things," said Paul, "were gain to me, those I counted loss for Christ" (Phil.3:7). And he maintained that attitude of mind despite all that he suffered as a prisoner in Rome, chained to a soldier, with death threatening every day. Don't you remember how he said, "Yea doubtless, and I count all things but loss for the excellency of the knowledge of Christ Jesus my Lord: for whom I have suffered the loss of all things, and do count them but dung, that I may win Christ" (Phil.3:8). There you have a man who had a desire for the heavenly country.

This desire shows itself particularly in the labour we expend in order to enjoy the Kingdom of God. It is true that we cannot be saved by our own works. It is equally true that we cannot be saved without works. "For as the body without the spirit is dead, so faith without works is dead also" (James 2:26). Hear what Paul says near the end of his journey: "I have fought a good fight, I have finished my course, I have kept the faith. Henceforth there is laid up for me a crown of righteousness, which the Lord, the righteous judge, will give me at that day; and not to me only, but unto all them that love his appearing" (2 Tim.4:7-8).

It is God himself who tells us that all must make a strenuous effort to reach the better country. "Strive to enter in at the strait gate: for many, I say unto you, will seek to enter in, and shall not be able" (Luke 13:24). "Give diligence to make your calling and election sure" (2 Peter 1:10). It is to the one who overcomes that Christ "will give to eat of the hidden manna, and will give him a white stone, and in the stone a new name written, which no man knoweth saving he that receiveth it" (Rev.2:17). He will "eat of the tree of life, which is in the midst of the paradise of God", and he "shall not be hurt by the second death" (Rev.

2:7,11). Christ will confess his name in the presence of his Father and his angels, and he will make him a pillar in the temple of God, and he shall no more go out of it, and he will write the name of his God on him, and the name of the city of his God, the new Jerusalem which comes down out of Heaven from his God, and he will write on him his own new name. He will grant him to sit with him on his throne, even as he himself has overcome and sat down with his Father on his throne. "He that hath an ear, let him hear what the Spirit saith unto the churches" (Rev.2:29).

> *0 that my spirit were ready,*
> *embroidered as though with gold,*
> *and clothed with the raiment*
> *that becomes the noble band;*
> *with my lamp lit*
> *and oil in my supply,*
> *to go in with him to the supper*
> *when he comes to call me.*

Who would not but strive and choose the road that leads to the better country?

Two English Sermons

Originally written some fifty years previously, both these sermons were preached in early 1976. They are as relevant today as they were then.

Sermon 4 – THE CONDITIONS OF SPIRITUAL POWER

While Peter yet spake these words, the Holy Ghost fell
on all them which heard the word. Acts 10:44

At the time of our Lord's Advent there existed amongst the Jews the same diversities of opinion and character as are found amongst ourselves at the present day. There were Sadducees then - as there are sceptics now - who doubted or disbelieved the truth as it had been revealed by Moses and the prophets. There were Pharisees then - as there are formalists now - who rested in the form whilst they denied the power of godliness. There were Pilates who asked, "What is truth?" (John 18:38) and Gallios who "cared for none of these things" (Acts 18:17). But there were also not a few whose hearts the Lord had touched.

Among the Jews we read of Zacharias and his wife Elizabeth "who were both righteous before God, walking in all the commandments and ordinances of the Lord blameless" (Luke 1:6). Among the Gentiles we read of the Ethiopian who came up to Jerusalem to worship (Acts 8:27), and of Cornelius, a Roman centurion, who was "a devout man, and one that feared God with all his house" (Acts 10:2). It is interesting to observe how these were prepared for greater things which God had in store for them. "Whosoever hath, to him shall be given, and he shall have more abundance" (Matt. 13:12).

In this chapter (Acts 10) we have the record of the first outpouring of the Spirit outside of Judea and Samaria, touching "the uttermost part of the earth" (Acts 1:8) for it came upon a representative Roman gathering. There was a little Pentecost that day in Caesarea. Pentecost at Jerusalem being the type and prophecy of Pentecosts all through the history of the Church of God. It was a kind of first-fruits - so we are justified in looking for other Pentecosts in history that shall not only be like the first Pentecost at Jerusalem but greater than that in results.

What is the greatest lack in the Church of God today? Is it not the lack of the power of the Holy Ghost? It is not the lack of ministers. We have thousands of them. It is not the lack of learning for we have many learned ministers. It is not the lack of churches for we have hundreds of thousands of them. It is not a lack of long Communion Rolls for some churches could drop a few off the Roll without any damage to the Church of God. What is the lack? Why, it is the lack of spiritual power. It is the lack of the anointing of the Holy Ghost.

In our days there is an increasing acknowledgement of the lack of power in the

Church of the Lord. In spite of all the multiplication of the means of grace, there is neither the power of the divine salvation in believers, nor the power for conversion in preaching, nor the power in the conflict of the church with worldliness, unbelief, and unrighteousness that we are bound to look for. The strength and power of the Church or of the individual believer is found solely in the Holy Ghost and therefore to rest on any other source of power is to lean on a bruised reed that will break.

What constitutes the power of a church? Numbers? God would rather have 7 consecrated men and women than 7,000 who are living according to the cause. Where lies the power of a church? In her wealth? No. The power of any church is in the Holy Ghost.

I

The question is, firstly, how is this power to be obtained?

Let us look at this incident [in Acts 10] and let us see what were the conditions of this power. Here we have power from above falling upon all those that heard the Word so that they were immediately brought to the saving knowledge of Jesus Christ and were baptised.

In the first place we have a messenger with a message. Notice who he was. He was Peter - a man, and a very frail man - a man that could not stand up before a maid and say, "I am Jesus' follower", but three times declared he did not know the man. Peter - saved by grace.

The Lord wants witnesses. What is a witness? It means 'to know'. Now, if you only know and have a voice to tell what you know, the Lord says "You can be my witness." If you do not know Christ, God will not have you for a witness, for you could not witness for Him - you have not anything to witness. Peter hazarded everything on the truth which he taught. He committed himself to the truth of the Gospel which he proclaimed. If this should fail him, he had lost everything, but this he knew would never fail. To him Christ was all - his joy, his heaven.

Callipas, an early missionary to China, said when the death sentence was uttered, "I have had no home but the world, no bed but the ground, no food but what Providence has sent me day-by-day and no object but to do and suffer for the glory of Jesus Christ, and for the eternal happiness of those who believe in His name" - utter devotion to Christ.

Samuel Rutherford tells us that in the little wood in Anwoth he received assurance from Christ that he would be a "chosen arrow hidden in His own quiver." But know, he adds significantly, this assurance is not kept but by watching and prayer.

II

Secondly, the people that heard the message. These hearers had a prepared mind for the message. Verse 33: "Now therefore are we all here present before God, to hear all things that are commanded thee of God." These words breathe the Spirit in when we should ever come to hear the Word. When we are conscious of being in His presence, when we recognise that the words are not a man's but "are commanded thee of God." And when we are all ears to listen and our whole will prepared to obey, we take the right attitude and may hope for a like blessing to that which fell on this small company.

No wonder that such an audience in such a disposition opened Peter's mouth. The eagerness of the audience is a large factor in the power of the speaker. Why, a man cannot help but preach when the people are praying for him with prevailing prayer to Almighty God, and when their hearts are opened to receive the Word and they can say in the presence of God, "Here we are before the Lord, all waiting to hear whatever is commanded thee of God." One reason for cold, ineffective sermons is found in cold, unexpectant hearers. Observe. God never forces the citadel of a hard heart. He will stand and knock but there must be a hand within to open, there must be a receptive mind and an obedient will or God enters not to take possession.

The message of Peter is a summary of Gospel truth, accompanied with its appropriate evidence. He intimates the personal dignity of Christ: "He is Lord of all" (v36). His humiliation as Jesus of Nazareth. His divine unction: "God anointed Jesus of Nazareth with the Holy Ghost and with power" (v38). His holy life: He "went about doing good" (v38). His death: "whom they slew and hanged on a tree" (v39). The fact that Jesus of Nazareth was crucified is not [truth to us however] unless we say with Peter that He died for our sin accordingly and rose again.

Finally, the sum and substance of the Gospel. "To him give all the prophets witness, that through his name whosoever believeth in him shall receive remission of sins" (v43). The Gospel is meant for the world. Christ alone gives remission of sins. Faith is the condition of receiving it. The same Gospel is preached in your ears.

Sermon 5 – GOD EXISTS

He that cometh to God must believe that he is, and that he is a rewarder of them that diligently seek him. Hebrews 11:6

Let us contemplate the true worship of God as He is presented to us here in connection with both aspects of a person's faith, namely, (1) he believes that God exists and (2) he believes that God is the rewarder of them that diligently seek him.

I

Firstly, God is. This should be our response to the affirmation which Moses heard - "I am that I am" (Exod.3:14). Reverently, we accept it and say, "God is". So convinced of this we say not that "there is a God" but "God is".

But, there are men - and they seem to have been numerous in David's time - who said in their hearts, "There is no God" (Ps.14:1; 53:1). And there are today three classes of people of whom this is still true. There is the bold atheist who denies that there is or can be any such Being as God. There is the agnostic who goes more than half-way and says he does not know that there is any such being. What he says is not that there is no God but that we cannot see Him, and are at a loss to perceive how anyone can know whether God is or not. The term agnosticism was invented by Huxley. His position was that he could neither affirm nor deny the existence of God. Accordingly, he coined the phrase 'agnostic' taken from the Athenian altar which Paul speaks of as dedicated to "the unknown God" (Acts 17:23), intending it to be antithetic to 'gnostic' - one who knows everything. Then there is the man who practically 'in his heart' and in the custom of daily life knows nothing of God, and thinks not of Him, and tries to believe that there is no God.

The first class claim to be omniscient themselves. To say that there is no God is an assertion without one iota of evidence. No one has any right to make this assertion till he has explored the whole universe, examined all its phenomena, and analysed all its forces.

The second class are in ignorance, partly because they wish to be so, or have put the evidence away, or have looked at it with such a prejudice and bias that they would not accept the proof which Reason and Conscience both give to the existence of God.

The third class are those who from an evil heart and life have closed their ears and soul and to whom God practically is not.

But is it so that God has left Himself without witness? And that there is no trace of Him to be found in the works of nature, as they are called, the works of creation and providence. The simple truth is that the world is full of facts which in the case of any human works of like kind would be conclusive evidence of an intelligent maker, and therefore the mind hastens to the conclusion that intelligence is at work here. Such marks of design are very numerous.

For ourselves, it is as sure as anything we know that "God is". It is inconceivable for us that the universe should be as it is without any supreme, intelligent, controlling Force or Power. And equally inconceivable that there should be moral life and a moral system, such as we see and know, without any Moral Perfection or Supreme Goodness.

But God has not left us wholly dependent on these services, valuable though they be, for our knowledge of His existence and of His character. For He has been pleased to give a revelation of Himself to man and of that revelation we have the record of His Word. The crowning revelation is made in the Person of Christ, but this revelation is open only to the Spirit-born; for no man "knoweth..the Father, save the Son, and he to whomsoever the Son will reveal him" (Matt.11:27).

Now, it is not merely in the existence of God as He is made known to us in the book of nature that faith believes, but in the existence of God as He is made known in the book of revelation, and especially in the revelation that He has given us of Himself in His Son. From these sources we learn that God is a spirit, infinite, eternal, and unchangeable in His being, wisdom, power, and holiness. This is the glorious Being in whose existence the true worshipper believes. He does not indeed see Him. But, in the exercise of faith on the testimony both of nature and revelation, he is as firmly persuaded that this God exists as if he saw Him with his bodily eyes. And it is because he has faith in the existence of this God that he comes unto Him or draws nigh to worship Him.

II

Let us now contemplate the true worshipper in connection with the other aspect of faith. "Faith is the substance of things hoped for, the evidence of things not seen" (Heb.11:1). The true worshipper, in the exercise of his faith, draws nigh to God believing that He is a rewarder of them that diligently seek Him. God is a renderer of reward to them that diligently seek Him.

Throughout the whole course of the revelation which God has given us of Himself he is ever presenting Himself as a rewarder of them that seek Him. Moses and Aaron among His Priests and Samuel among them that call upon His name. They called upon the Lord and He answered them. Moses "had respect to the recompense of the reward" (Heb.11:26).

He has made Himself known as the hearer of prayer. He has not said to "the seed of Jacob, Seek ye me in vain" (Isa.45:19). On the contrary, He has even laid it as a duty upon all who know about Him that they call upon Him. And when those who know about Him do not call upon Him He charges that against them as sin.

In the Old Testament we have Him swearing by Himself that He has no pleasure in the death of the wicked but that the wicked turn from His way and live. But in the New Testament we have Him doing what is still more impressive. There He reveals Himself as so loving the world that He gave His only begotten Son (John 3:16). There He reveals Himself as ready to adopt us as His children and to become a Father unto us (Eph.1:5; 2 Cor.6:18). There, too, we are exhorted to come with boldness (Heb.10:19).

This is a subject that is fitted to give both direction and encouragement to those who are exercised about the deepest questions that can engage man's thoughts; and are ready to cry out from the bottom of their heart, "Oh that I knew where I might find Him!"

Many persons have no understanding of the depths into which some are plunged by these questionings even as to the very existence of God, or of the joy that is felt by them when they get to the settled conviction that "God is".

Rabbi Duncan was one of those who experienced for years the misery of doubt, and then felt the joy of belief. We have the record of the change in the following remarkable words from his own lips. He says, "When I was convinced that there was a God I danced on the Brig o' Dee with delight tho' I had fear He might damn me" Now, if there be anyone here having such doubts there is nothing in the universe of such consequence to Him as to have those doubts solved.

God has given a revelation of Himself. Multitudes can testify that they have found Him. He declared that He is a rewarder of them that diligently seek Him - that seek Him out. What then remains for those who are in doubt but that they seek Him - and that they seek with the earnestness, the humility, the prayerfulness, and the continuousness which alone are reasonable in a search after God. Doubters of all men ought to be the most intensely in earnest. But how often are they the very reverse? How little are they on their knees. Let them try coming through Christ. If they don't, where is their earnestness?

But, turning now from all these, I think there is much here for the direction and encouragement of those who are not troubled with doubts. May not the young find direction and encouragement here. To you, dear friends, the Lord has said, "They that seek me early shall find me" (Prov.8:17). You little know how unspeakably precious it would be for you thus to find the Lord early - from how much sorrow it would save you - how much peace and joy it would secure to you, even in this world. Life can never become at all what it ought to be until you find the Lord and I mean by that until you get so to know the Lord Jesus Christ that you will trust Him as your Saviour and give yourselves entirely to Him.

He is willing to make Himself thus known to you, but our text tells you that you must seek Him out diligently. Believe firmly that He will make Himself known to you if you thus seek Him and with this as a settled conviction give Him no rest until you find Him, taking this text for your guide and encouragement.

Acting on it, no limit can be placed to the blessings that you might receive from Him. How high, how holy, how useful, how happy might your life be were you to act from this day forward upon this text. What a truly noble career might be before you. But may not all of whatever age find direction and encouragement here.

APPENDICES

Appendix I

Fiftieth Anniversary Speech

What follows is a transcript of the speech given by the Rev. Kenneth Gillies at his Jubilee Service in Partick Gardner Street Church of Scotland on May 24, 1974.

"I think I can say without guile that I thank you - my heart thanks you - for your presence here this evening. And I would like very warmly to thank you for this expression of your kindness.

"It is one of the prerogatives and pleasures of age to look back and remember the days of old. How well I remember the ordination and induction service which made me a pastor of this congregation. It fell to the late Dr. Roderick MacLeod of the Highlands and Islands Mission to preach. The late Rev. William Jardine, Belhaven Church, presided and gave the charges. I was introduced to the congregation by the Rev. Alexander Murray of Beauly. I then went at once into my work and had the joy to find myself surrounded by a sympathetic people.

"The work of a city minister is certainly strenuous, but I have been very happy in it. No minister could have had a more loyal backing than I have had. No man could have wished for a happier situation to serve Christ in. I had no real difficulty in this congregation with the people, I always found them frank and kindly, generous and receptive. I am quite satisfied that my being with them proceeded from the Lord. He has honoured us together

"We have seen His hand at work, confirming the Word with signs following. This church has been a Bethel to many. We have seen the power of God evinced among people in bringing sinners to sit at the feet of Jesus and give Him the throne of their hearts. It was in this church that I was brought to the Lord myself, so that the very dust thereof is dear to me. *Now, for my friends and brethren's sakes, Peace be in thee I'll say. And for the house of God our Lord, I'll seek thy good always (Ps. 122:8-9).*

"There is only one place in all the world where your life and mine can attain the full maximum of blessedness and usefulness. It is for us to find out that place and get there. We dare not lay out our lives at less than their highest design.

"When I look back upon all the way the Lord hath led me during the fifty years of my ministry, and the great measure of health I have enjoyed so as to be able to prosecute my labours without a single break or interruption, I desire first of all to express my deepest gratitude to God for His unbounded goodness. And to raise afresh my stone of Ebenezer saying "Hitherto, hath the Lord helped me" (cf 1 Sam.7:12). On the other hand, when I look back upon the defects of my ministry I feel deeply humbled. I know I have fallen short of my aim.

"It was charged against a certain minister, otherwise popular with his people, that his prayers were not comprehensive enough - they did not cover all his congregation. Next Sunday he set this right by remembering the whole of his congregation: young and old; rich and poor; sick and well; on sea and on land - in prison and out of prison! That seemed to include them all! At all events he had no more complaints!

"I may say with a good conscience that I have regularly visited all the members of the congregation; attended upon the sick and dying; and kept myself so much in touch with all the members and adherents that I have had few complaints on account of the want of pastoral visitation. Great changes of course I have seen, as you can realise. We have not been without our sorrows, we never shall be while here, but let us thank God for His unfailing goodness.

"The highest fruit of a ministry is not numerical or financial. It is seen in the number of regenerated men and women in lives which are radiant and beautiful with the beauty of Christ. Therefore let us lift up our hearts in adoring gratitude to God for health and guidance throughout the years and give ourselves more wholeheartedly to Him and to the service of His Kingdom in the coming years. I thank you all for your presence and for this gift which you have given to me."

Appendix II
Excerpts from Tributes
a) Rev. A.I. MacDonald at the Memorial Service in Gardner Street on July 28, 1976.

For I am now ready to be offered and the time of my departure is at hand. I have fought a good fight, I have finished my course, I have kept the faith: henceforth there is laid up for me a crown of righteousness which the Lord the righteous judge will give me at that day. 2 Tim.4:6-8

These words present us with a picture of the soldier who has served fully and faithfully and looks triumphantly to his Master's commendation. We pay our respects with heavy hearts, nevertheless with thanksgiving to God for a soldier of the cross to whom these words are applicable and appropriate...

The Apostle writes to Timothy of the good fight using a word that means a beautiful fight - a delightful fight - an enjoyable pursuit despite the enemy. There is no doubt that Mr. Gillies enjoyed the Christian life to the full. "For him to live was Christ" and he expressed his desire 'to die in harness' as he put it. God granted his desire.

The word 'good' used here by Paul is the same word used by Jesus in commending Mary's service when she broke the alabaster box of ointment to anoint Jesus. It was sacrificial service stemming from love for her Master. It was criticised service, nevertheless it was - and is - a memorial to her. The service of the soldier we miss was unstinting and its fragrance reached out in Christ-like manner to many lives and it is his memorial today. "The righteous", says the Psalmist, "shall be in everlasting remembrance."

In this good fight our late minister wrestled not with carnal weapons. God gave him so clearly to understand that prayer allied with the Sword of the Spirit, which is the Word of God, were alone mighty to pull down the devil's strongholds. The Lord confirmed to him the victory that overcomes the world - the faith of Jesus Christ dwelling in him. He was blessed with souls for his hire and Gardner Street continues to this day as a place where people meet Christ as Lord and Saviour. The Lord favoured him with the fulfilment of these words from Psalm 92:- "Those that be planted in the house of the Lord shall flourish in the courts of our God, they shall still bring forth fruit in old age."

...Mr. Gillies' pastoral concern never failed and as I spoke to him last week his interest in people and his zeal for soul-winning were as vibrant as ever. He sympathised with those who suffered and rejoiced in the joys of God's blessings, but supremely he shared the joys of those who came to know salvation in Christ Jesus.

God was pleased to use him in praying and preaching to the end. The prophet reminds us that, "They that be wise shall shine as the brightness of the firmament; and they that turn many to righteousness as the stars for ever and ever" (Dan.12:2-3).

...We may summarise his life as we hear the Lord speaking about His faithful servant at the end of Psalm 91:

"Because he hath set his love upon me, therefore will I deliver him:
I will set him on high because he hath known my name.
He shall call upon me, and I will answer him:
I will be with him in trouble;
I will deliver him, and honour him.
With long life will I satisfy him,
And shew him my salvation."

It is with triumphant thanksgiving for the privilege He granted us through the Rev. Kenneth Gillies that we who knew him as a friend and minister would by grace look unto Jesus, the author and finisher of our faith, and press toward the mark for the prize of the high calling of God in Christ Jesus. May the Lord grant us to be thus minded.

b) Rev. T.M. Murchison in the October 1976 edition of *Na Duilleagan Gaidhlig*. A translation follows on.

Ard agus èasgaidh 'na phearsa; sìmplidh, dùrachdach, agus druidhteach mar shearmonaiche, dìchellach neo-sgìtheil mar aoghaire; còir, càirdeil, companta, iriosal agus uasal 'na uile ghluasad - b'e sin Coinneach MacGill-Iosa, neach mu'n robh e da-rirìbh fìor gun do "ghluais e maille ri Dia agus cha robh e ann, oir thug Dia leis e."

Rugadh e air a'Chomraich - "Comraich Mhaol Rubha" - an 1887. B'ann an cladh na Comraich, dlùth do'n uaigh aig Maol Rubha, a chàirich sinn na bha bàsmhor dheth. Bha sinn ann, ann an Eaglais Chamus-tearach agus mu'n uaigh, càirdean as gach ceàrn, maille ri a dhaoine fhéin, muinntir na Comraich. An là roimh siud bha sluagh mór cruinn 'na eaglais fhein am Partaig - an coimhthional a bu chaomh leis agus leis am bu chaomh e, agus càirdean eile. Bhathas a' caoidh gun d'fhalbh e, ach aig a' cheart ám ag àrdmholadh an Tighearna air son gach beannachd a bhuilicheadh air ar brathair agus air sluagh do-àireamh trìd a fhianais agus a shaothrach.

..Cha ruig mise a leas feuchainn ri meas a chur air luach a shaothrach am Partaig - cha b'urrainn mi no neach eile. Taisgte an iomadh cridhe tha cuimhne agus buidheachas. Agus chan ann a mhàin am Partaig. Bha ar caraid tric a' cuideachadh aig Orduighean thall 's a bhos, agus, 'nam bheachd-sa co-dhiùbh, b'e am ministear Gàidhealach a b'fheàrr aithne am measg nan Gàidheal 'nam latha-sa. Cha b'ann a mhàin am measg sluagh Eaglais na h-Alba a bha aithne agus meas air Mgr Coinneach, ach an Eaglaisean eile mar an ceudna.

..Chuala mise, is mí 'nam bhalach òg, mu Choinneach MacGill-Iosa fada mus fhaca mi e. Bha Seonaidh MacCalmain (misionaraidh Chaol-reithe), bràthair m'athar, còmhla ris anns a' Chablach Rìoghail, agus bha meas mór aige air. Chuir mi aithne phearsanta air, is mi 'nam oileanach, o chionn faisg air leth-cheud bliadhna, agus anns an ùine fhada sin bha sinn tric a' coinneachadh agus a' cuideachadh a chéile. Bidh sinn uile 'ga ionndrainn.

..Tall and lithe in person; simple, earnest and penetrating as a preacher; diligent and tireless as a pastor; kind, friendly, companionable, humble and noble in all his ways - that was Kenneth Gillies, a person concerning whom it was indeed true that "he walked with God, and was not, for God took him."

He was born in Applecross - "Applecross of Maree" - in 1887. It was in the churchyard of Applecross, not far from Maree's grave, that we laid to rest all that was mortal of him. We were there, both in the church in Camusterrach and at the graveside, friends from far and near, along with his own folk, the people of Applecross. The previous day there had been a large gathering in Partick - the congregation he loved and who loved him, and other friends. His passing was lamented, but at the same time there was much thanksgiving to God for all the blessings that had been bestowed on our brother and an innumerable people through his witness and labours.

..I need not try to estimate the worth of his work in Partick - neither I nor anyone else could. Stored in many a heart there is remembrance and gratitude. And not only in Partick. Our friend frequently assisted at Communion seasons far and near, and, in my view, he was the minister best known among Highlanders during my time. It was not only within the Church of Scotland that Kenneth was known and respected, but in other churches as well.

..When I was a young lad, I heard about Kenneth Gillies long before I met him. My uncle, John Murchison (missionary at Kylerhea) had served with him in the Royal Navy and had a high regard for him. I got to know him personally during my student days, nearly fifty years ago, and during that long time we frequently met and assisted each other. We shall all miss him.

c) Rev. Roderick MacDonald, his former assistant (1942-44), wrote this tribute in the same edition of *Na Duilleagan Gaidhlig*. Once again, there is an English translation.

Rinn am bàs beàrna mhór 'nar measg mar Ghàidheil an uair a thug e air falbh an t-Urr. Coinneach Mac'Ill-Iosa... Ach ann an seagh, saoilidh sinn nach e am bàs a thug air falbh e, ach Prionnsa na Beatha do an robh e cho dìleas ré a bheatha fhada a chaidh a bhuileachadh air.... Agus cia mór an ionndrainn a bhios anns a' choimhthional do an tug e ùine cho fada de a bheatha, agus am measg nan ceudan, no nam mìltean, d'an tug e cuideachadh is comhfhurtachd ré a mhinistrealachd. Feumaidh mise aideachadh gur mi fhìn aon diùbh sin, air dhomh a bhith am fhear-cuideachaidh aige fhad 's a bha mi am oileanach ann an Colaisde na Trianaid an Glaschu. Nithear iomradh air an Urramach Coinneach mar shearmonaiche is gu sònraichte mar aoghaire, agus cha bu chòir 'obair ann an Taigh-Eiridnidh a' Chnàmhuin a dhì-chuimhneachadh, ach is ann mar dhuine is mar charaid, saoilidh mi, a bhios cuimhne air gu sònraichte. Chan 'eil fios agam có a bu dluithe a bha air cridhe an Urramaich Coinneach, a chiomhthional an Glaschu no sgìr a bhreith agus àraich, a' Chomraich, ach is ann 'san sgìre sin a chuartaich e Bòrd Suipear an Tighearna air son na h-uair mu dheireadh, agus is ann a fhuair a chorp an fhios dheireannach, am feadh, tha sinn a' creidsinn, a sheòl a spiorad gu buadhmhor a shealbhnachadh na foise a dh'fhàgadh-fa chomhair sluagh Dhé. Is maith, da-rìreabh, a rinn thu, a dheagh sheirbhisich mhùirnich agus dhìlis, imich a steach do dh'aoibhneas do Thighearna. Gun togadh an Tighearna dhuinn fàidhean is fianaisean is teachdairean eile de leithid ar caraid gràdhach a tha a nis air a thoirt uainn.

Death created a great gap amongst us Gaels when it took from us the Rev. Kenneth Gillies...But in a sense we feel it is not death that has taken him but the Prince of Life, to whom he was so faithful during the long years granted to him... How great will be the sense of loss in the congregation to which he devoted such a long portion of his life, and amongst the hundreds, or thousands, to whom he gave help and comfort throughout his ministry. I have to confess that I myself am one of these, having been an assistant with him when I was a student at Trinity College in Glasgow. Kenneth will be remembered as preacher, and especially as pastor, and the work he did in the Cancer Hospital ought not to be forgotten, but I believe that it is as a man and as a friend that he will be remembered particularly. I do not know which was closer to Kenneth's heart, his congregation in Glasgow or the place of his birth and upbringing in Applecross. It was there that he participated in the Lord's Supper for the last time, and it was there that his body found its last resting-place, while, we believe, his spirit took flight victoriously to possess the rest that has been prepared for the people of God. Well, indeed, have you done, dearly beloved and faithful servant; enter in to the joy of the Lord. And may the Lord raise up for us prophets and witnesses and messengers of the stamp of our beloved friend who has been taken from us.

d) The August 1976 bulletin of the Glasgow Presbytery, *The Bush*.

The death of Kenneth Gillies brought to an end one of Scotland's most remarkable ministries. Not only was he the longest serving minister in the Church of Scotland but all his ministry had been spent in one congregation . . . Although in his 90th year, he still worked days which often began before nine in the morning and did not end until very late at night. Over and above this he ministered to a congregation which had more services than most in the land.

During the 52 years that his ministry in Gardner Street lasted Kenneth Gillies became almost a legendary figure not only with the Highland Community in Glasgow but also throughout the North of Scotland. A man of tremendous energy he managed to be not only a first-class pastor to his own widespread congregation in Glasgow but also a travelling preacher of considerable reputation throughout the North of Scotland. . .

The crowded church in Gardner Street on the day of his funeral was an ample testimony to the fact that a man born in another century was still, even at the time of his death, influencing for good people of a very different generation. Gardner Street Church and Partick – and even Glasgow – are not going to be quite the same without him.

Appendix III

Gardner Street Elders 1924-76

a) Rev Kenneth Gillies' first Session Meeting - June 1924

Donald MacVean	- joined from Govan St. Columba's 1898; elder 1900; died 1932?
Malcolm MacAskill	- from Skye; member 1897; deacon 1898; elder 1902; Deacons' Court Clerk 1902-04/22-24/34-36; Session Clerk 1924-25 and 1934-54; Congregational (Central Fund) Treasurer 1915-21/24-27/28-54; Church Officer 1918-19/40-43; died 1954
Donald John MacLennan	- from Harris; member and deacon 1898; Deacons' Court Clerk 1898-1902/24-34 Congregational Treasurer 1906-10; Session Clerk 1925-33; died 1934
Duncan MacKellar	- from Argyll; joined from Govan St. Columba's 1904; deacon 1904; elder 1907; died 1935
Donald MacGregor	- from Lewis; member and deacon 1907; elder 1910; died 1948
Donald William Maclean	- from Lewis; member 1905; deacon 1907; elder 1910; died 1968
Donald Gray	- member 1905; deacon 1913; elder 1923; emigrated to New Zealand 1924
John Thomson	- member 1912; deacon 1913; elder 1923 Deacons' Court Clerk 1916-18; suspended from Kirk Session in 1926 following allegations against Malcolm MacAskill; died 1929
Donald MacKinnon	- joined from Govan St. Columba's 1919; elder 1923; died 1934
Peter MacArthur	- from Argyll; newsagent; member 1920; elder 1923; church auditor 1924-32; died 1947
John Cunningham	- joined from London Road 1923; elder 1923; left church 1928

In absentia

Alexander Kerr	- joined from Govan St. Columba's 1903; elder 1904; died 1935
John Macrae	- member 1901; elder 1910; Deacons' Court Clerk 1918-21; died 1924?
Donald J. MacDonald	- member 1908; deacon 1910; elder 1919; died 1958
Allan Campbell	- joined from Cranston Hill 1912; deacon 1913; elder 1923; left for America 1925

b) Elders admitted during period of Kenneth Gillies' ministry

| 1928 | Donald Macdonald | - | from Bernera, Lewis; policeman;member 1925; left for Arrochar 1935 |

1928 Donald Macdonald — from Bernera, Lewis; policeman;member 1925; left for Arrochar 1935

     Donald Macrae — from Lewis; police detective; member 1914; Maintenance of Ministry Treasurer 1929-34; died 1934

     John MacLeod (White Street) — from Skye; member 1909; deacon 1910; Foreign Missions Treasurer 1935-43; Gaelic precentor; died 1954

1928 Donald Beaton — member 1925; left church 1929

     David Campbell — member 1920; left church 1929

1931 Lachlan Mackinnon — from St Kilda; member 1926; deacon 1928; died 1963

     Duncan Henderson — from Glasgow; member 1929; Church officer 1936-38; choir member; died 1946

     Donald Mulholland — from Islay; joined from St. Columba's 1929; retired 1945; died 1952

1935 Johnnie Macleod (Govan) — from Lewis; worked on Clyde ferries; deacon 1931; Church Officer 1943-47; church auditor 1944-48; left for Ness in 1967; died 1971; father of Murdo, current Church Officer

     John MacLeod (Overnewton) — from Staffin, Skye; retired to Skye 1964; died 1988

     Kenneth Macdonald — from Shawbost, Lewis; member 1932; died 1958

     Malcolm Macdonald — from North Uist; 'The Captain'; fruiterer in Whiteinch; member 1933; church auditor 1936-54; Deacons' Court Clerk 1936-54; Congregational Treasurer 1954-55; died 1955

     Donald MacQueen — from St. Kilda; member 1926; died 1962

1941 William Macleod — member 1939

     Kenneth Morrison — from Laxay, Lewis; member 1935; church officer 1947-57; Foreign Missions Treasurer 1944-54; fatally injured at zebra crossing going home from prayer meeting in 1973

     William Smith — from Lewis; member 1940; church auditor 1943-59; died 1965;

1942 Neil Macdonald — from North Uist; member 1941; died 1951

b) Elders admitted during period of Kenneth Gillies' ministry (cont)

1949 Donald Macdonald   - from Scarp; policeman; member 1939;
Gaelic precentor; left for Harris 1949;
later Clerk to Harris District Council; died 1987;
daughter, Tina McLellan, Gardner Street member.

       Malcolm Morrison   - member 1946; left 1955

       Murdo Nicolson   - from Uig, Lewis; worked for Clyde Trust;
member 1948; church auditor 1953-57;
Foreign Missions Treasurer 1954-66;
WFO Treasurer 1972-74; returned to Lewis 1974;
died 1986

       Samuel McBurney   - from Northern Ireland; member 1942;
Church auditor 1952-56;
Deacons' Court Clerk 1954-62;
Session Clerk 1954-64;
Congregational Treasurer 1957-64; died 1965

       Angus MacDonald   - from Durness, Sutherland; member 1938;
Maintenance of Ministry Treasurer 1950-66;
Temperance Representative 1956-59; died 1972

1954 Calum Ian MacDonald   - from Uig, Lewis; worked on the Renfrew ferry;
died 1981

       Roderick Mackay*   - from Tolsta Chaolis, Lewis; deacon 1949;
Church Officer 1958-61; left for Fort William 1965;
now living in Inverness

       Malcolm MacLennan   - from Scalpay; worked for MacBraynes;
member 1950; Gaelic precentor;
Church auditor 1960-64; WFO Treasurer 1968-70;
Congregational Treasurer 1970-72; died 1972

       Angus Morrison   - from Harris; sea-captain; member 1944;
died in a Saturday evening meeting in 1962
having just spoken.

1960 Archibald Macleod*   - from Harris; police superintendent; member 1951;
deacon 1954; left for Harris 1977; now in Inverness

       Murdo D MacLennan   - from Scarp; worked for Clyde Trust; member 1953;
deacon 1954; Church Officer 1981-84;
died day before leaving for Lewis in 1988;
father of Ruaridh, current Gardner Street
Session-Clerk

       David Kilpatrick   - from Glasgow; member 1955;
Church auditor 1960-71;
Deacons' Court Clerk 1962-72;
Church organist 1963-72;
Session Clerk 1964-72; retired to Harris 1972;
died 1995

b) Elders admitted during period of Kenneth Gillies' ministry (cont)

1960 Donald MacAulay — from Point, Lewis; worked for Clyde Trust; member 1944; deacon 1949; Gaelic precentor; died 1987; father-in-law of Finlay MacRitchie, current elder

Angus A. MacDonald* — from Bernera, Lewis; policeman; member 1952 deacon 1954; returned to Lewis 1964

1965 Norman Macleod (Victoria Park) — from Arnol, Lewis; deacon 1960; Roll-Master 1971; Congregational Treasurer 1972-80; returned to Lewis 1988; died 1993

Hector Gillies — from Glasgow; dentist/shepherd; member 1955; WFO Treasurer 1967; left for Applecross 1985; died 1994; younger son of Rev K. Gillies

1965 Donald Livingstone* — from Applecross; joiner; member 1955; Sunday School Superintendent 1955-71 and 1974-79; Fabric Committee Convener 1965-79; left for Applecross 1979

Neil MacKillop — from Berneray, N. Uist; member 1962; died 1992

Roderick MacKillop — from Berneray, N. Uist; member 1961; died 1980; brother of Neil

Donald MacLeod* — from Kilmuir, Skye; member 1957; retired to Skye 1989

Donald John Smith* — from Shader, Lewis; member 1955; deacon 1960; Church Officer 1961-66; church auditor 1971-75; Gaelic precentor; Roll-Master 1974-76; left for Lewis 1976

Finlay MacRitchie* — from Barvas, Lewis; car dealer; deacon 1960; Fabric Committee 1965 -

1970 Kenneth Paterson* — from Barvas; engineer; member 1967; Sunday School Superintendent 1971-74; left to work in Lewis 1974

Kenneth MacDonald* — from Applecross; retired lecturer in Celtic; member 1958; deacon 1965; Deacons' Court Clerk/Session Clerk 1972-92

Murdo Smith — from Glasgow; member 1961; deacon 1965; church auditor 1968-70; Roll-Master 1970-71; died 1971; son of William Smith, elder 1941-65

Duncan Martin* — from Harris; accountant; member 1958; deacon 1965; Congregational Treasurer 1965-70; left for Edinburgh 1970

Norman Macleod (Penilee) — from Ness, Lewis; worked for Rolls-Royce; member 1964; died 1977

b) Elders admitted during period of Kenneth Gillies' ministry (cont)

1970   Calum Iain Morrison   -   from Uig, Lewis; worked for Clyde Trust; member 1964; died 1991

       Duncan Maclean   -   from Shader, Lewis; worked for Clyde Trust; member 1964; died 1984

       John MacLeod   -   from Ness; member 1964; Church Officer 1966-81; died in Partick Station going home from evening service; father of Iain, current Gardner Street elder

       John Morrison   -   from Harris; member 1966; Church Officer 1966; died 1971

       George Miller   -   from Glasgow; accountant; member 1958; deacon 1965; Congregational Treasurer 1955-57; Fabric Committee 1965-86; died 1986

       Malcolm MacQuarrie   -   from North Uist; member 1955; left for Duntocher 1979; died 1990

* *indicates still living.*

Appendix IV
Gardner Street Minister's Assistants 1924-76

Date	Name and Place of Origin	Subsequent Place(s) of Service
1924-25	James Riach	unknown
1925-26	Murdo MacLennan, Lewis	Carloway (1931-64)
1926-28	Hector Munro, Glasgow	Kilbirnie (1933); Lochranza (1940); Law (1948); Bowling (1957-63)
1928-30	John Bryce (two terms)	unknown
1930-32	Angus MacKenzie, Applecross	Assynt (1933-71)
1932-33	Murdo MacSween, Scalpay	Kinloch (1933); Royal Navy (1941); Strath (1944); Govanhill (1951-60)
1933	Ernest Martin	unknown
1935	Harry MacKinnon, Skye	Knock (1937); Creich (1963-70)
1936	James Grant, Skye	Portknockie (1946); Ythan Wells (1952-54)
1936	Andrew Clark	unknown
1936-38	Donald MacLeod, Berneray	Kilmuir/Paible (1938); Dingwall (1946); Portree (1951); Fairlie (1968-79)
1938-39	Donald MacDonald, Lewis	Melness/Eriboll (1939); Kirkhill (1946-53)
1939-42	Alex John MacLeod, Lewis	Portree (1945); Iraq (1951); Brussels (1959-74)
1942-44	Roderick MacDonald, N. Uist	Stornoway (1946); Insch (1967-83)
1944-47	Robert Carmichael, Glasgow	Arran (1948); Newtyle (1966); Kilmelford (1975-91)
1947-48	Ian Cameron	missionary, Argyll
1948-50	John Honeyman, Falkirk	Faith Mission; Shetland (1957); Rhynie (1967-74)
1950-52	Robert Reid, Linlithgow	Faith Mission; Dundee (1958); N. Ireland (1963); Glasgow Cranhill (1969); Mossgreen/Fife (1984-85)
1952	Kenneth MacLeod, Lewis	Glenelg (1955); Plockton/Kyle (1959); Dairsie/Fife (1964); Stornoway (1969-85)
1952-62	John Farquhar	Faith Mission (Director)
1960-61	John Campbell, Lewis	C.O.S. missionary
1963-64 } 1969-75	Raymond McKeown, Glasgow	Open Air Mission; Belfast (1982-85)
1964-66	William Duguid	died soon after
1969-73	John Ferguson, North Uist	Cross (1973); Portree (1980-)
1970-76	John Morrison, Scalpay	retired C.O.S. missionary
1975	Thomas McGlade, N.Ireland	Faith Mission; Scripture Press, Cumbria

Appendix V
Gardner Street Members 1924-76

Information as to when people became members of Gardner Street was initially extracted from the Kirk Session Minutes. These numbers were then grouped into 4-year bands. **P.O.F.** indicates those who joined by profession of faith; **Cert** refers to those who joined by transfer of certificate from another congregation. Numbers in brackets relate to names listed on the Communicants' Roll.

Date	P.O.F.	Cert	Total	
1924-28	62	72	134	
1929-32	56	53	109	(100)
1933-36	40	47	87	(87)
1937-40	43	23	66	(67)
1941-44	31	34	65	(59)
1945-48	27	17	44	(47)
1949-52	31	26	57	(48)
1953-56	48	20	68	(77)
1957-60	34	7	41	(49)
1961-64	15	6	21	(44)
1965-68	22	8	30	
1969-72	25	9	34	
1973-76	17	2	19	
Totals	456	327	783	(795)

Some interesting points arise. The discrepancies in the **Total** column between the Kirk Session and Communicants' Roll records show that my grandfather could not have been too concerned about keeping church membership details meticulously accurate! Illustrating this, there is no mention in either source as to when six of the Gardner Street elders appointed during his ministry actually joined the church - if they ever did!

Furthermore, my own father's name appears in the Session Minutes when he became a member in 1948, but his name is not found at all on the Communicants' Roll. The reverse situation applies to my late uncle. Hector's name appears on the Roll in 1955, but no reference is made in the Session Minutes to him having ever become a member.

Appendix VI

Three Gaelic Prayers (with translation)

In his memorial tribute in the *Stornoway Gazette*, the Rev. T.M. Murchison referred to Kenneth Gillies' ministry as being "steeped in prayer." These three short examples were written to be broadcast on radio and give a brief insight into the recurrent themes at the heart of his lifestyle of prayer. In each case a translation follows.

Prayer 1

O Thigearna Cruith-fhear chrioche na talmhainn eisd a diugh ri ar n-athchuinge agus ar neadar ghuidh air son nan uile dhaoine. Beannaich ar càirdean 's ar luchd-daimh am fad agus am fagus. Gu robh sinne agus iadsan air ar ceangal suas an ceanglaichean na beatha maille ri Crìosd.

Tha sinn ag ùrnuigh air son an t-saoghail bhochd anns a bheil sinn a gabhail còmhnuidh. Tha aingidheachd air teachd gu àirde mhòr. Tha an cruthachadh uile ag osnaich agus ann am pein gu leir gus an am seo.

Thigeadh do rìoghachd-sa. Luathaich an là anns am bith uachdaranachd aig Criosd o fhairge gu fairge agus on amhuinn gu ruig criochaibh na talmhainn. Moladh am pobull thus a Dhè, moladh gach pobull thu. Beannaich gu saoibhir, tha sinn a' guidhe ar dùthaich anns na làithean caraideach anns a bheil sinn beò. Gleidh ar Ban-rìgh le d' ghràs agus deonaich do ghliocas do ar cinniuil a tha an arainbhe 's an ùghdarras 'nar tìr chum gu caith sinn ar beatha gu foisneach agus gu siochail anns an uile dheadhachd agus chiatach. Deonaich do chòmhnadh 's do chuideachadh an diugh do chlann na trioblaid de gach dùil. Thoir comhfhurtachd dhoibhson uile tha ri bròn neart do'n-anmhuinn 's do cho chomunn don mhuinntir a tha aonaranach.

Beannaich a Dhè ghrasmhoir t-aobhar is d'Eaglais fein an diugh. Thoir fianais anns gach aite do fhocal na beatha 's na firinn. Ath-bheriach t-obair chum 's gu'm bi do shluagh air an ùrachadh gu mòr, agus a mhuinntir a tha fhathast a taobh a muigh air a toirt a steach do chearcal beannaichte na slàinte. 'S na h-uile a tha sinn ag iarraidh 's ann an ainm Chrìosd. Amen.

O Lord, Creator of the ends of the earth, hear today our prayer and intercession for all men. Bless our friends and kinsfolk both near and far away. May they and we be bound up together in the bonds of life with Christ.

We pray for the needy world in which we live. Evil has risen to a great height. The whole creation groans and travails in pain until now.

May Thy kingdom come. Hasten the day when Christ shall have dominion from sea to sea, and from the river to the ends of the earth. "Let Thy peoples praise Thee, O God; let all the people praise Thee." We pray that Thou wilt richly bless our land in those unsettled days in which we live. Defend our Queen by Thy grace, and grant Thy wisdom to our leaders who have high position and authority in our land, that we may lead a quiet and peaceable life in all godliness and honesty. Give Thy help and succour to those who mourn, strength to the weak, and Thy companionship to those who are lonely.

Gracious God, bless today Thine own cause and Thy Church. Bear witness in every place to the Word of life and truth. Revive Thy work, so that Thy people may be greatly refreshed, and those who are still outside may be brought in to the blessed circle of salvation. And all we ask is in the name of Christ. Amen.

Prayer 2

A Dhè ghràsmhoir, bha thusa 'nad ionad-còmhnaidh dhuinn o linn gu linn, o bhith-bhuantachd gu bith-bhuantachd is tusa Dia. Rinn thusa nèamh agus an talamh le d'mhòr chumhachd agus le d' ghàirdean sìnte mach chan eil nì sam bith tuilleadh as cruaidh ort; oir do Dhia tha na h-uile nì comasach.

Dh' àithn thu dhuinn ar coimhearsnaich a ghràdhachadh mar sinn fèin agus eadar-ghuidhe a dhèanamh airson nan uile dhaoine. Builich oirrn spiorad nan gràs agus nan athchuingean chum gun dèan sinn gnothach riut as leth muinntir eile.

Beannaich na h-uile bhuineas duinn agus a tha sinn a' gràdhachadh. 'S e dùrachd ar cridhe agus ar n-ùrnuigh ri Dia air an son gum bitheadh iad air an tèarnadh. Tha sinn a' cuimhneachadh 'n ad làthair a tha ann an trioblaid. Naomhaich dhaibh uile dhèiligean do fhreasdal agus uile shtrithean do spioraid. Thoir comhfhurtachd dhaibhsan a tha ri bròn. Tarraing iad ann am fagus riut fèin. Ullaich iadsan a tha dlùth do dhorsaibh bàis airson àm a siubhal agus fritheal gu pailt dhaibh slighe a-steach do 'n dùthaich as fheàrr.

Cuimhnich oirrn mar rioghachd anns na làithean brònach anns a bheil sinn beò. Ann an corraich làimh tròcair. Dòirt a-mach do spiorad air gach uile fheòil chum gum bi daoine air an bioradh nan cridhe agus gun tionndaidh iad ris an Tighearna agus gun tòisich iad ri gairm air ainm an Tighearna. Agus gach nì a tha sinn ag iarraidh 's ann air sgàth an Tighearna Iosa Criosd. Amen.

Gracious God, thou hast been our dwelling place in all generations; from everlasting to everlasting thou art God. Thou hast made the heavens and the earth by thy mighty power and by thine outstretched arm. There is nothing too hard for thee, for to God all things are possible.

Thou hast commanded us to love our neighbour as ourselves, and to make intercession for all men. Grant to us the Spirit of grace and of supplication so that we may plead with you on behalf of others.

Bless all those who are connected with us and whom we love. It is our heart's desire and prayer to God for them that they might be saved. We remember in thy presence those who are afflicted. Sanctify to them all the dealings of thy providence and all the strivings of thy Spirit. Give comfort to those who are sorrowing. Draw them close to thyself.

Prepare those who are drawing near to the gates of death for the time of their departure, and minister to them an abundant entrance into the better country.

Remember us as a nation in those dismal days in which we live. In wrath remember mercy. Pour out thy Spirit on all flesh, so that men may be pricked in their heart and turn to the Lord and call on his name. And all that we ask is for the sake of the name of the Lord Jesus Christ. Amen.

Prayer 3

A Dhè naoimh, is tusa ar carraig, ar daighneach, adharc ar slàinte, ar Slànuighear. Cuidich leinn a bhi beò anns an t-saoghal seo mar is còir dhuinn. Chan eil sinn an seo ach airson ùine ghoirid; uime sin tha sinn ag iarraidh gun caitheamaid aimsir ar cuairt ann an eagal naomh agus gum bitheadh gràs an Tighearna air a fhrithealadh dhuinn gach là. Tha tha a' gealltuinn do gach neach air a bheil eagal an Tighearna gu stiùir thu iad le do chomhairle, gun dèan thu dorchadas na sholas rompa, gun nochd thu dhaibh an t-slighe anns an còir dhaibh imeachd, gun treòraich thu iad air slighe dhìrich agus gun toir thu iad gu tìr an ionracais. Thubhairt thu, "Feuch tha mise maille ribh a ghnàth, gu deireadh an t-saoghail." Stiùir sinne agus bì maille rinn air sgàth Chriosd. Amen.

Most holy God, thou art our rock, our fortress, the horn of our salvation, our Saviour. Help us to live in this world as we ought. We are here but for a short time; therefore we pray that we may spend the time of our sojourning here in holy fear, and that the grace of the Lord may be ministered to us each day. Thou dost promise to all those who fear the Lord that thou wilt guide them with thy counsel, that thou wilt make the darkness light before them, that thou wilt show them the way in which they ought to walk, that thou wilt direct them on a straight path, and bring them to the land of righteousness. Thou hast said, "Behold, I am with you always, even to the end of the world." Guide us and be with is for the sake of Christ. Amen.

Notes

Chapter 1 - Applecross Background

1. The name Culduie is probably derived from Cùil-duibh, the black nook, according to W.J. Watson Place-Names of Ross and Cromarty (Inverness: Northern Counties Publishing Co., 1904)

2. Cited by Kenneth D. MacDonald, Session Clerk, Gardner Street Church of Scotland, on the occasion of the 50th Anniversary of Kenneth Gillies' ordination and induction, May 24, 1974.

3. F. Thompson The Crofting Years (Edinburgh: Luath Press, 1984) p49

4. Rev. Norman Morrison, writing in 1949, makes reference to these evictions as to "the most rocky and forbidding promontories by the sea shore where arable land is scarce, broken and uneven" in The Third Statistical Account of Scotland Vol. XIII ed. A.S. Nather (Edinburgh: Scottish Academic Press, 1987) p316

5. Kenneth D. MacDonald (1980) 'The MacKenzie Lairds of Applecross' in Transactions of the Gaelic Society of Inverness Vol. LIV 1984-86 p440

6. The New Statistical Account of Scotland Vol. XIV (Edinburgh: Wm. Blackwood & Sons, 1845) p100

7. Census Returns 1841 (District No. 58) Reproduced with the kind permission of the Registrar General for Scotland, New Register House, Edinburgh

8. D.T. Gunn Applecross, Wester Ross: Development or Decline? (Aberdeen University: Unpublished M.Litt. Thesis, 1978) pp70-73

9. School Board of Applecross Minutes 1873-1919 File 5/2/1 p188 Inverness Library

10. Ibid. p181

11. Ibid. p188

12. Ibid. p191

13. Captain William Murchison Master in Sail (Navigator Books, 1995) p16. Copies can be obtained from his daughter, Mary Murchison, Ribhuachan, Lochcarron

14. Ibid. p20

15. Ibid. p21

16. Ibid. pp35-36

17. Third Report of the Congested Districts Board for Scotland (1901) Appendix IV p15 National Library of Scotland, Edinburgh

18. SRO AF 42/1440 File 2220, 'Application for grants in aid of the construction of footpaths on the south coast of Applecross'. Letter, dated January 15, 1903, to the Congested Districts Board. West Register House, Edinburgh.

19. Ibid. Report, dated July 30, 1903, of a sub-committee of the Western District Committee, Ross & Cromarty County Council. Each man in the benefiting townships was to give four days free labour due to their inability to pay anything towards the cost of the footpaths.

20. Ibid. Western District Committee Report, April 23, 1904.

Chapter 2 - New Directions

1. Burgh of Partick: Constables Register, Record and Defaulters Book Glasgow City Archives, Mitchell Library

2. A.A. Woolsey 'Time for the Beat' in Life Indeed The Magazine of the Faith Mission, Edinburgh, No. 1025 (1974) p90

3. Ibid.

4. The Gardner Street Communicants' Roll records that he actually joined the church in April 1909, although the Kirk Session Minutes do not list him as one of the new members. The Roll also states that his membership was transferred to Applecross in May 1910 but, once again, this cannot be confirmed as the Camusterrach congregation's records do not mention any transfer. It would seem rather strange for him to have lifted his lines in the light of his going to BTI that same autumn.

5. Bible Training Institute Report 1910-11 p3 with kind permission of the Glasgow Bible College Association

6. BTI Report 1912-13 p6

7. BTI Report 1910-11 p5

8. Seek & Save: A Record of Work for 1910 p1 The 37th Annual Report of the Glasgow United Evangelistic Association, Glasgow Bible College

9. Ibid.

10. SRO CH3/983/6, United Free Church Highlands and Islands Committee Minutes, September 26, 1911, Register House, Edinburgh

   Rev. John Murray, from Garrabost in Lewis, preceded Kenneth Gillies as student assistant in the High U.F. Church, Aberdeen, 1918-22. After becoming minister in Lybster that year, he moved to Strathconan in 1928 and then to Oban in 1932. Married to Jessie Morison, daughter of the Rev. Neil Morison, Carloway, he died in 1936 aged fifty-four.

   Rev. Neil Munro was from Easdale, Oban. He was student assistant at Partick Gardner Street prior to being ordained and inducted to Strathy in 1922. In 1928 he headed east to Latheron before moving to Hopeman in 1934 where he remained for the next twenty years until demitting his charge.

   Details on individual ministers, with kind permission of the Church of Scotland, come from the following three sources:

   The Fasti of the United Free Church of Scotland 1900-29 (London: Oliver and Boyd, 1956) ed. J.A. Lamb

   Fasti Ecclesiae Scoticanae 1929-54 Vol. IX (London: Oliver and Boyd, 1961) ed. J.A. Lamb

   Fasti Ecclesiae Scoticanae 1955-75 Vol. X (Edinburgh: Saint Andrew Press, 1981) ed. D.F.M. MacDonald

11. SRO CH3/983/6, U.F. Church Highlands and Islands Committee Minutes, October 24, 1911

12. A.A. Woolsey op. cit. p90

Chapter 3 - Naval Service and Aberdeen Studies

1. A.A. Woolsey op. cit. p91

2. Information from the Admiralty Library, 3-5 Great Scotland Yard, London SW1A 2HW. The sinking of the *Louvain* by the German U-boat resulted in the loss of 7 officers and 217 ratings. Many of the complement were Maltese.

3. Sankey's Sacred Songs & Solos No. 529 (Marshall, Morgan & Scott, London)

   Verse 2 reads: *Down in the valley with my Saviour I will go,*

                        Where the storms are sweeping and the dark waters flow;

                        With His hand to lead me I will never, never fear:

                        Dangers cannot fright me if my Lord is near.

4. Archie Robertson spent most of his life in Tain where he was a well-known businessman. I am indebted to his niece, Miss Anne Bell, a member of Gardner Street, for providing me with a copy of his reminiscences.

5. SRO CH 3/983/6, U.F. Church Highlands and Islands Committee Minutes, September 16, 1919

6. The Aberdeen University Calendar 1921-22 p181 (A.U. Press)

7. AUL MSU 1013/4, University of Aberdeen Degree of M.A.: List of Candidates (1918-22), Department of Special Collections and Archives, King's College

8. A.U. Calendar 1921-22 p228

9. Information on graduates of Aberdeen University extracted from:

   Roll of the graduates of the University of Aberdeen 1901-25 (with supplement 1860-1900) ed. T. Watt (A.U. Press, 1935)

   Roll of the graduates of the University of Aberdeen 1926-55 (with supplement 1860-1925) ed. J. MacKintosh (A.U. Press, 1960)

   Roll of the graduates of the University of Aberdeen 1956-70 (with supplement 1860-1955) eds. L. Donald & W.S. MacDonald (A.U. Press, 1982)

10. A list of Kenneth's fellow-students at Christ's College is found in The Church College in Aberdeen (A.U. Press, 1936). A copy of this book is in Aberdeen Central Library.

    The Rev. Donald Campbell was ordained and inducted to Croy, near Inverness, in April 1924. After five years there, followed by a similar period in Dundee, he went to Edinburgh. In 1947 he accepted a call to the parish of Glass and Strathbogie. He died in 1951 aged fifty-two.

11. The Rev. Angus Duncan was ordained and inducted to Sorbie, near Wigtown, in 1926. Three years later he moved to Kilmeny, Islay, staying there until 1936 when he went to Ladybank in Fife. In 1947 he demitted his charge. A short spell in Duns followed between 1950-53. His son has edited his detailed observations of life on Scarp in the book: A. Duncan Hebridean Island (Tuckwell Press, 1995)

12. The Rev. Lachlan Macleod was ordained and inducted to Duirinish in 1927. In 1930 he accepted a call to Knock. Five years later he made the short trip to Stornoway St. Columba's where he remained until 1945 when he moved to Glenurquhart.

13. The Rev. Richard Robertson spent most of his years in Aberdeen and the North-east. The Rev. Robert Smith's longest period was in Coatbridge between 1931-54. The Rev. Arthur Wallace was ordained and inducted in 1926 to Blochairn, near Glasgow, from where he retired in 1968. He died in 1980.

14. Kenneth's class placements are found in the following A.U. Calendars:

    a) 1921-22 pp 242, 628; b) 1922-23 pp 623, 653-654

15. A Centenary of Witness (1981) The Old Aberdeen Mission

16. Dr William Emslie, Aberdeen, in a letter to my father, August 1976.

17. Aberdeen Daily Journal July 14, 1922

18. The following volumes of The Aberdeen University Review contain short obituaries:-

    AM - XLIII (1969-70) p212; MM - XL (1963-64) p399; KM - XLI (1965-66) p57

    Department of Special Collections and Archives, King's College

19. A. Gammie The Churches of Aberdeen (Aberdeen Daily Journal Office, 1909) pp138, 192-193. In the wake of difficulties following the establishment of the United Free Church in 1900, St. Columba's was allocated to the Free Church. Both sites are now licensed premises.

20. SRO CH 3/501/2, U.F. Church Presbytery of Lochcarron, April 8, 1924

Chapter 4 - Gardner Street Introduction

1. W. Ewing Annals of the Free Church of Scotland 1843-1900 Vol. II (Edinburgh: T & T Clark, 1914) p106

2. Cited by Rev. David Barr, Chaplain to the Royal Infirmary, on the occasion of the 50th Anniversary in 1974

3. I.R. MacDonald Glasgow's Gaelic Churches (Edinburgh: Knox Press, 1995) p55

4. Introduction to Partick Free Gaelic Church Session Minutes, January 1880. The following Gardner Street Church records were referred to:-

Deacons' Court Minutes	Volume 1: April 1889 - January 1905
	Volume 2: February 1905 - June 1938
	Volume 3: September 1938 - October 1965
	Volume 4: November 1965 - September 1986
Kirk Session Minutes	Volume 1: January 1880 - January 1920
	Volume 2: January 1920 - October 1976
Communicants' Roll Book	Volume 1: January 1880 - January 1906
	Volume 2: January 1906 - January 1926
	Volume 3: January 1927 - January 1966
	Volume 4: January 1966 - January 1978

5. I.R. MacDonald op. cit. p56 notes that "this was the George Macleod who had been active as secretary of the Glasgow Gaelic Mission from 1855 when he was minister of Duke Street. However, in 1868 he had resigned from Duke Street after the Presbytery had commenced disciplinary proceedings against him because of his reported alcoholism. After his resignation from Duke Street, the Highland Committee

employed him from time to time on various assignments and he continued in Partick as the agent of the Highland Committee until 1882 when the local management committee requested his removal."

6. In January 1880 there were twenty-seven names on the Communicants' Roll.

7. The title deeds were signed on February 13 and 15, 1886, and deposited with the General Register of Sasines on March 12. The original trustees were Roderick Maclean, grocer, Cranstonhill; John Cameron, carpet planner, 17 Overnewton Square; Archibald Stewart, factor; Malcolm Paterson, joiner, 4 Church Street; Donald Robertson, shipwright, 14 Mansfield Street; David Alexander, blacksmith, 26 Squire Street, Whiteinch.

    The Deacons' Court Minutes for August 1889 show that the pavements which the church was responsible for were still not complete.

8. Communicants' Roll Book Volume 1 pp.63, 75, & 94

9. Deacons' Court Minutes, November 25, 1898

10. Ibid.

11. Deacons' Court Minutes, November 8, 1898. My italics.

12. Deacons' Court Minutes, February 14, 1899

13. The Deacons' Court Minutes for November 25, 1898, proposed that a sum of £2,000 out of an estimated cost of £4,500 (excluding fees) be raised by the congregation - a figure equivalent to £115,000 in today's (1998) money. (Comparative monetary values both here and elsewhere supplied by the Business & Technical Department, Aberdeen Central Library)

14. Story told by Angus M. Macdonald, elder, in the 1970 edition of The Gard (Magazine of the Young People's Group in Gardner Street)

15. Deacons' Court Minutes, May 7, 1901. This was £1,000 less than three years earlier.

16. SRO CH/981/1, Minutes of the Church & Manse Buildings Committee, February 28, 1905, p158. The cost of the church is given as £3,202.12s.10d. In applying for a grant, £826 had already been raised by the congregation together with £750 from Presbytery and £200 from the Ferguson Bequest. It was believed the church could seat 750; the front hall 400. Membership was 175; adherents 251. Income was £230 per annum; the debt £100.

17. Kirk Session Minutes, April 20, 1905. The opening of the new halls in 1902 had seen the establishment of concurrent Gaelic and English morning services. The latter in the small hall for "young people and others."

18. Partick Gaelic United Free Church Bazaar Guide Book 19th - 21st October 1905 'Statement and Appeal' p3 Mitchell Library, Glasgow

19. Deacons' Court Minutes, December 20, 1905

20. Kirk Session Minutes, April 27, 1908

21. Kirk Session Minutes, September 23, 1912. The Minutes for September 9, 1912, show that 155 voted for hymns with 54 against, and 143 voted for instrumental music with 68 against.

22. I.R. MacDonald op. cit. pp75-76

23. It is worth noting that in a congregation which was - and is - regarded primarily as a Highland or Gaelic Church, that of those surnames on the Roll of Honour at least 40% are not of Highland origin e.g. Broadfoot, Buckingham, Hancock, Harris, Spalding, Spittal, Woodhouse. The most common names to appear are Cameron (eleven times) and Maclean (nine times).

24. Deacons' Court Minutes, January 17, 1919

25. Deacons' Court Minutes, November 23, 1923

26. Deacons' Court Minutes, June 2, 1924

Chapter 5 - Of Marriage and Ministry

1. Rev. Arthur Wallace was one of four guest preachers invited to take a service on Sunday, May 26, 1974, to commemorate Kenneth Gillies' fifty years in Gardner Street. He also took part in the Memorial Service two years later. At the evening service on February 26, 1978, the Rev. Mr Wallace was once again in the Gardner Street pulpit to mark the unveiling of the Memorial Plaque to his lifelong friend.

2. Later renumbered 148, the Deacons' Court Minutes, September 9, 1924, urged "that electric light be installed as speedily as possible."

3. Deacons' Court Minutes, November 23, 1923

4. Kirk Session Minutes, February 7 and 26, 1929. The vote was 9 to 2 in the Session; and 175 to 18 in the congregation.

5. On June 23, 1957, a baptismal font was dedicated to her memory in the church.

Chapter 6 - Days of Grace and Glory

1. The Rev. John Macleod was a student assistant between 1943-45 at St. Columba's - Copland Road. He became a Chaplain in the Royal Navy before leaving for an appointment with the Presbyterian Church of Canada in 1948. He was inducted into a charge in Edinburgh in 1961 and then became minister of Kilmore and Kilbride Oban Old in 1967. He died in 1997, only a matter of months before the Rev. Roddy MacDonald.

2. Letter from Donald John Smith, April 1996

3. A.A. Woolsey Channel of Revival A biography of Duncan Campbell (Edinburgh: Faith Mission 1974) p121

4. John Farquhar, Faith Mission Superintendent, and later Scottish Director, was assistant in Gardner Street between 1952 and 1962.

5. The Rev. K. MacDonald became minister of Snizort North in 1965 before moving to Applecross in 1978.

6. The Rev. J. M. Smith was minister in South Uist for seven years before being inducted to Lochmaddy, North Uist, in 1963.

7. Church Hymnary (Revised edition) No.248 (Oxford University Press)

8. Alexander's Hymns, No 3 Hymn 39. (London and Edinburgh: Marshall Bros.)

Chapter 7 - The Miles Mount Up

1. Letter from Donald John Smith, April 1996
2. One of three tributes to appear in the Stornoway Gazette on August 14, 1976. The Rev. John Ferguson has been minister in Portree since 1980.
3. Letter from the Rev. John G. Fraser, May 1996. He was inducted into MacGregor Memorial in 1960. He died in August, 1998.
4. Taken from a pamphlet to commemorate his 40th Anniversary in Gardner Street, April 1964.
5. Jim Handyside Portrait of a Master Craftsman (Belfast: Ambassador Productions, 1987) tells the story of Raymond McKeown.
6. In the 1971 edition of *The Gard* (No.2) a translated letter from the boy, Koo Tingchen, appears. The name Kenneth Gillies is bracketed beside it.
7. Deacons' Court Minutes, October 6, 1969

Chapter 8 - Last Days

1. Verse written around 1935 in Alexander's autograph book by his father
2. Both men had been recent Moderators of the General Assembly of the Church of Scotland: the former in 1969 and the latter in 1971. The Very Rev. T.M. Murchison was for thirty-five years until his retiral in 1972 minister of St. Columba's - Copland Road (in 1966 linked to become St. Columba's - Summertown). He was editor of the Gaelic Supplement of the *Life and Work* from 1951 until 1980. He died in 1984.
3. A transcript of his speech appears in Appendix I
4. Psalm 91:1-2 reads as follows:

> *He that doth in the secret place*
> *of the Most High reside,*
> *Under the shade of him that is*
> *th'Almighty shall abide.*
> *I of the Lord my God will say,*
> *He is my refuge still,*
> *He is my fortress, and my God,*
> *and in him trust I will.*

5. Letter from Mrs Mary Peckham (neé Morrison), March 1996

Photo Acknowledgements

AKG Collection – pp 2, 3, 5, 13 (top), 15, 37, 43, 54, 58

W.B. Anderson, Aberdeen – p 32

Fox Photography (J&T Fox), Glasgow – Cover: Frontispiece; pp 44, 53

Imperial War Museum, London – p 16

David Kerr – p 24

W. Macleod, Stornoway – p 13 (bottom)

MacMahon, Aberdeen – p 21

Ralston, Glasgow – p 46

Scottish Press Agency Limited, Glasgow – p 50

Studio Scotland, Glasgow – p 59

Weir's Studio, Glasgow – pp 10, 34

The Author – p 63